Great Rail-Trails of the Northeast

The Essential Outdoor Guide to

26 Recreational-Biking Trails

and Their Railroad History

by Craig Della Penna

New England Cartographic
Amherst, Massachusetts 1995

D0967624

Cover design and photos by Bruce Scofield, with Boston & Maine Railroad, Pacific type locomotive on the Lexington Branch at Bedford, Massachusetts Depot April 10, 1956. (Photo by Donald Robinson from the Walker Transportation Collection of the Beverly Historical Society)

> **Due to changes in conditions, the use of information in this book is at the sole risk of the user.**

10   9   8   7   6   5   4   3   2   99   98   97   96

Dedicated to the youngsters in my life;
Genevieve, Jake, Joey, Kaleigh, and Stephanie.

So that they may have safe places to ride their bikes, and to gain an
appreciation for what was once there.

Preface

I am a professional in the transportation field, the manager of Railroad Distribution Services, an inter-modal facility owned by the Pinsly Railroad Company. One of my customers, New England Cartographics, is a publisher of outdoor recreation maps and guides that cover the New England region. The owner of N.E. Cartographics, Chris Ryan, was in my office one day in February, 1994, and noticed that I had a copy of *The Lost Railroads of New England* by Ronald Dale Karr. We started to discuss abandoned railroad right-of-ways, and the growing interest in the Rail-to-Trails Movement.

It became apparent that, between the two of us, we could not think of a single informative guide on the subject of rail-trails (abandoned railroads which have been converted to multi-use paths, managed by state or local agencies, and designed to be safe and fun -- *safe* being the operative word here.). Chris and I decided that such a book might generate some interest. He contracted with me to do the research and write a manuscript. I had no idea of the scope of the project or what I'd find along the way.

First I made contact with the managers of about 50 rail-trails throughout New England. Then my wife Kathy and I bought a pair of fat-tired mountain bikes. We purchased very inexpensive, popular brand-name bicycles to see if they would hold up as well as some of the pricier types. Starting in April, 1994, we set out to bike, photograph, and catalog as many rail-trails as we could on weekends. Many moons had passed since we were last on bicycles, but gradually we were able to do 30-to-40 miles on gravel without feeling badly fatigued.

We found that some trails were not safe enough to put into a book aimed at beginners (like us). Kathy doesn't like to cross 100' bridges without decks over deep rivers, so we eliminated those trails. There were some trails where we kept trying to find a safe or practical way around major obstacles, such as highways that were built across the rail bed with no provision for the rail-trail user to pass through. Altogether we did more than 1300 miles of biking on this project, a challenge for us, but not much by the standards of some of the "terminator" types that we met during this endeavor.

Although we intended to do all 50 of the New England trails in one season, this was logistically impossible. This first edition of *Great Rail-Trails of the Northeast* has twenty-six trails. We will be continuing on in 1996. Look for us, we'll be out there.

Acknowledgments

The following people had a part in the completion in this book. For their contributions, I am deeply in their debt.

Irv and Isabel Baker, Stan Beauregard, Don Blake, Bob Buck, Bob Ceccolini, Bob Champagne, Bill Coutu, Mark Cutler, Dan Dickinson, Craig Vincent della Penna, Catherine Dimitruk, Jim DiMaio, Joe Durham, Wayne Fieden, John Folsom, Stephen Fontaine, Wes Flierl, Wayne Goldwaithe, Paul Gray, Edith Griffin, Marilyn Griffin, Greg Gordon, Kathleen Haniffy, John Hankins, Paul Hansen, Marita Hartshorn, Joe Hickey, Jack Johnson, Ronald Karr, George Kahale, Steve LaBonte, Ginny Leslie, Marc Levine, Kevin Lynch, Alan Massey, Alan McClennen, Betty Newhouse, Steve Nicolle, Dan O'Brien, Tim O'Donoghue, Kevin O'Malley, Bill O'Neil, Rollie Ortegon, Phillip Pearo, Bill Penn, Don and Diana Poplaski, Jeff Powell, George Plumb, Scott Ramsey, Preston Reed, Paul Shaw, Scott Ramsey, John A. Roderick, Andy Rubel, Chester Russell, Monique Russell, Chris Ryan, Gary Salmon, Bruce Scofield, Alan Socea, Marjorie Silver, Bob Spoerl, Richard Symmes, Larry Tallman, Gerard Toner, Valerie Vaughan, Robert Walker, Robert Whalen, Larry Whipple, Buddy Winiarz, Elise Wood.

I am especially thankful to John Hankins, Bill Penn, and Al Massey for their assistance in the compilation of information on the Hop River State Park Trail.

Special thanks go to Chris Ryan, Bruce Scofield, and Valerie Vaughan for their invaluable assistance and patience.

If I have forgotten to mention someone, it is unintentional.

We welcome any suggestions, comments, or corrections to this book.
Please send them to the author:
c/o New England Cartographics, P.O. Box 9369, North Amherst, MA 01059
or the E-mail address is Rail trail @ AOL.com

Contents

Locater Map
for the Great Rail-Trails of the Northeast

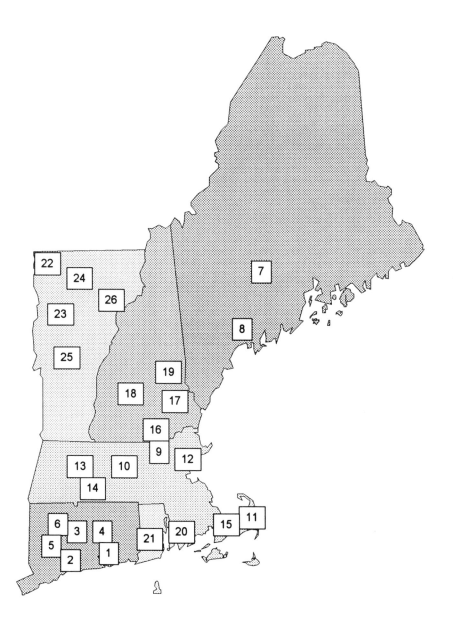

QUICK REFERENCE RECREATION USE TABLE

TRAIL #	STATE	NAME OF TRAIL	HIKE	ROAD BIKES	MT. BIKES	HORSES	WHEEL CHAIR	IN-LINE SKATES	FISHING	X-C SKI	SNOW MOBILES	ATVs
#1	CT	AIRLINE	X		X	X			X	X		
#2	CT	FARM. CANAL	X	X	X		X	X		X		
#3	CT	FARM. VALLEY	X	X	X		X			X		
#4	CT	HOP RIVER	X		X	X			X	X		
#5	CT	LARKIN	X		X	X				X		
#6	CT	STRATTON	X		X				X	X		
#7	ME	JAY	X		X	X				X	X	X
#8	ME	S. PORTLAND	X	X	X		X	X		X		
#9	MA	AYER	X		X	X			X	X		
#10	MA	BARRE	X		X	X			X	X	X	
#11	MA	CAPE COD	X	X	X	X	X	X		X		
#12	MA	MINUTEMAN	X	X	X		X	X		X		
#13	MA	NORTHAMPTON	X	X	X		X	X		X		
#14	MA	NORWOTTUCK	X	X	X		X	X	X	X		

TRAIL #	STATE	NAME OF TRAIL	HIKE	ROAD BIKES	MT. BIKES	HORSES	WHEEL CHAIR	IN-LINE SKATES	FISHING	X-C SKI	SNOW MOBILES	ATVs
#16	NH	MASON	X		X	X				X	X	X
#17	NH	ROCKINGHAM	X		X	X			X	X	X	X
#18	NH	SUGAR RIVER	X		X	X			X	X	X	
#19	NH	WOLFEBORO	X	X	X	X	X	X	X	X	X	
#20	RI	EAST BAY	X	X	X		X	X	X	X		
#21	RI	TRESTLE TRAIL	X		X	X			X	X	X	
#22	VT	ALBURG	X		X	X			X	X	X	
#23	VT	BURLINGTON	X	X	X		X	X	X	X		
#24	VT	CENTRAL VT.	X	X	X	X			X	X	X	
#25	VT	D&H	X		X	X				X	X	
#26	VT	WELLS RIVER	X		X	X				X	X	

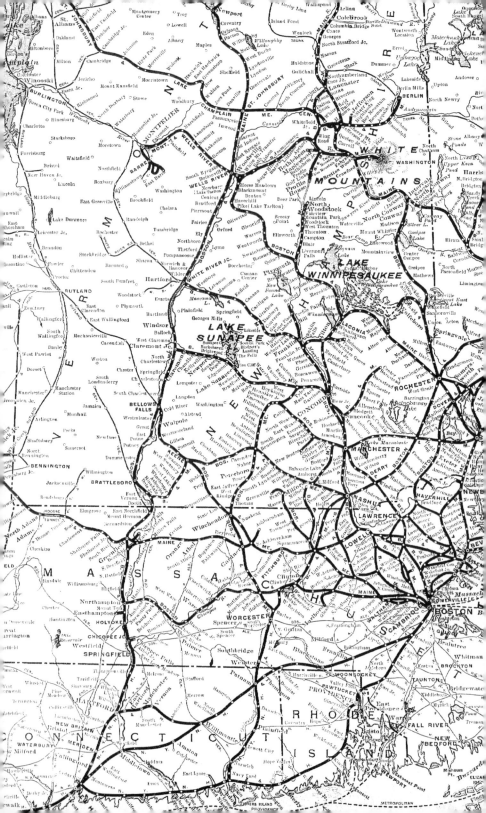

Introduction

Where did rail-trails come from?

At the beginning of this century, nearly every city and town had a railroad passing through. It was a great status symbol to have a railroad and communities often bid against one another to entice the railroad to come to town. In many cases, palms were greased to facilitate a deal.

Looking at a map of New England from this period, one can see the complex entanglement of railroads going anywhere and everywhere. From a high-water mark of about 270,000 miles of track around World War I, the system has shrunk to today's total of about 130,000 miles. This shrinkage was in large part due to the arrival of the automobile and the flexibility of trucks as a competitor.

A surprising fact to most people is that the railroads are economically stronger today than in any period since the Second World War. This is in part true because of a law called the Staggers Rail Act of 1980. One component of this law made it easier for railroads to abandon unprofitable branches.

In the years prior to Staggers, it was a bureaucratic nightmare to dump lightly used branch lines. Before the Federal government's Interstate Commerce Commission would grant the formal abandonment, the petitioning railroad had to appear at a series of public hearings and present its case to the locals concerned about their loss of a railroad connection. It was not uncommon for the ICC to deny abandonment because one shipper would object to the loss of service. In many cases, the whole process took years to complete.

Once Staggers was enacted, it took only a matter of months to dispose of the unwanted and unprofitable branches. Staggers' streamlined process allowed an additional option; instead of abandonment, a sale to a qualified "short-line" operator could be considered. Because of hands-on, local management, such lines could be marketed as a place where shipping problems would be solved quickly, and customer service became the order of the day. Short lines or feeder lines now represent about 20% of the trackage in the country and are a successful alternative to abandonment.

In the early 1980s, so many branches were being abandoned and broken-up by encroaching abutters, that in 1983, Congress passed an amendment to the National Trails System Act. This instructed the ICC to allow abandoned rail lines to be "railbanked," or set aside for use in the future as a transportation corridor, while being used as a trail in the interim.

The controversy surrounding rail-banking resulted in many lawsuits brought by private property owners who objected. Many believed that once railroads were abandoned, the property should revert to the abutters. Ultimately, the United States Supreme Court decided the issue *(Preseault v. United States)* in favor of the recreation community.

In this case, Paul and Patricia Preseault, land developers in the Burlington, Vermont area, sued over the ex-Rutland right-of-way that ran by their house. The Court ruled that rail banking is constitutional and a legitimate exercise of the power of the Interstate Commerce Commission. However, the case was remanded to a lower court in order to decide if the Preseaults deserved any compensation for the loss of the use of their land.

In 1993, Claims Court Judge Christine Nettesheim denied compensation, ruling that the easements were given for railroading purposes, and that "the use to which the easements were put, evolving from railroading to rail banking, is consistent with preserving the easements for rail use." This decision removed the cloud over the nationwide issue of rail banking and spurred the acquisition and development of rail-trails all over the country.

The *Rails-to-Trails Conservancy* (RTC), formed in 1985 as a Washington, DC-based, non-profit membership and lobbying organization, was set up to educate the public as to the benefits of linear parks and to monitor impending abandonment so local or state agencies can act quickly to secure ownership. RTC can now claim to have a hand in the acquisition or improvement of over 600 rail-trails across the country, which translates to over 7,000 miles. The 500th trail in the nation's inventory is included in this book. It is known as the Minuteman Trail. Ironically, the Minuteman also set a record in terms of the number of years from start to completion - 18 years. Persistence pays off.

Why rail-trails?

Neither the RTC nor this book advocates in any way the abandonment of the nation's economically viable rail infrastructure. Only the railroad companies themselves can determine the profitability of their own lines. If there are not customers on-line to serve, then the railroad ceases to perform its prime function as a business; and that is to make money.

The RTC advocates recycling abandoned lines into "greenways" or linear parks that can see another life as corridors for passive recreation, linking together communities across the nation.

Information on membership in the RTC is listed in the Sources, at the end of this book.

[photo 3.5]

Northbound Vermonter Amtrak at Norwottuck Junction, Massachusetts. This contemporary scene is taken from the same spot as the archive photo on page 117 and is adjacent to the new (1996) Norwottuck Trail Extension about 1/2 mile past Station Rd.

The advantage a railroad has over other modes of land transportation is based on principles of physics. A train with steel wheels rides on steel rails which are laid on broad sweeping curves and gentle grades. This is much more fuel-efficient than the number of trucks required to carry the same load over highways.

The same principles are what makes a bike trail on an old rail-bed much more efficient and fun to travel. There are no traffic lights, automobiles, sharp turns, or steep climbs. The paved trails are especially attractive to disabled people in wheel-chairs and parents with strollers. These places are ideal for cross-country skiing and snow-mobiling in winter. In urban areas they provide a bit of recreation space that is appreciated by city folk as well as the businesses that are located "on-line." In some cities, the rail-trails have become a passive commuter highway with people biking or walking to work.

Rural trails provide tourists and dollars, a stimulus to ancillary businesses such as bed and breakfasts and tour groups. Some of the rural trails also provide a unique perspective on the local wildlife.

Bob Spoerl, of the State of New Hampshire's Department of Resources and Economic Development, pointed out one feature that makes rail-trails special. There are many instances where a pond or other body of water is bisected by the trail. The wildlife found there is usually inaccessible, being in the middle of the pond, but from the trail can be viewed up-close and personal.

You do not have to travel far to appreciate the benefits of the rail-trail experience. In our encounter with people all over New England, one theme that continued to strike home was how surprised people were to find such interesting old places and buildings right there under their noses, just waiting to be rediscovered. Support for the historic preservation effort in this country is being enhanced by the growth of rail-trails.

Lonely depots and stations, some with semaphore signals that no longer communicate with trains, are metaphors for a language no longer spoken. Some of these buildings are being restored to their former grandeur; not to provide shelter while awaiting transport to another place, but instead to provide a gateway to another time. Sampling the trails within this book can mean more than just walking or biking in solitude. You also have the chance to connect with the path of the country's optimism and vibrancy.

Rails are in place over the Hop River, just north of the New England Central Railroad junction at Mackey's in Willimantic, Connecticut.

How to Use This Book

The rail-trails are organized in alphabetical order by state. Each state has a heading page that lists all its rail-trails and gives a basic map showing the approximate location of trails within that state. Each map is complemented by an old (circa 1925) Boston & Maine Railroad route map that shows all major routes in New England (The B & M and allied railroads are shown in bold lines, while the routes of B & M's competitors are shown in much thinner lines.).

Each Rail-Trail description in this guide is set up like the example below:

Norwottuck Rail-Trail *(the official name of the trail)*

Endpoints: Elwell State Park, Damon Road, Northampton, Massachusetts to Station Road, Amherst, Massachusetts
(These are the normally accepted endpoints which make for a safe trip. They may not represent the entire abandoned railroad branch, but they are the safe or approved sections.)
Location: Hampshire County, Massachusetts towns of Northampton, Hadley, and Amherst.
(This is the county, state, or states where the trail is located, along with the towns or cities that it passes through.)
Length: 9 miles
*(This is the length of the trail **one way** measured on a bike odometer. This length may differ from that listed in other sources or printed matter.)*
Surface: Asphalt
(The materials used to make the trail surface.) These also include:

Gravel; which is coarse sand that drains well and locks together to provide a firm surface;

Sand; loose beach sand material that tends to be soft and swallows up tires;

Cinder; coal by-product left over after burning. Gray to dark gray in color, this was used by the railroads years ago because of its unlimited availability and its unique ability to prevent the growth of weeds. This is a good firm surface.

Ballast; Large stones, usually about 2-3 inches in diameter, on which the original track structure was placed. This type of surface is not much fun to ride a bike on.

Uses: *(The following icons represent the different uses that are approved for the trail. The ones listed below represent the entire range of icon types and descriptions used in this guide, not just the Norwottuck Trail's allowed uses.)*

bicycling

fishing

mountain-bike-riding

cross-country skiing

walking, running

roller-blading, roller skating

horseback riding

ATVs (all-terrain vehicles)

snowmobiling

wheelchair access

Contact:
Daniel O'Brien, Bikeway & Trail Planner, Dept of Environmental Management 100 Cambridge Street Room 104, Boston, MA 02202 (617-727-3160 Ext. 557) *(This is the person who can be contacted to provide local color and information. Sometimes it is an official government manager or it may be a resident that has volunteered to accept calls, even at their home. Either way, this is the person to write or call about the trail.)*

Local Resources for bike repairs/rentals:
(The bike shops listed here are the ones that were near the trail and willing to be included in the book at the time of publication. It should be noted that this type of business is prone to being seasonal or having a high turnover, so be alert for changes.)

The main body of the trail history follows now. The information presented is not meant to be the last word on that trail's former owners. It will, however, give a flavor of why it was there and the reason for its abandonment.

The odometer-based mileage guide is next. This will show important geological and man-made features along the way. Having an odometer on your bike on a Rail-Trail is not required, but will increase your enjoyment of the trail and will prevent your missing some of the small pieces of railroad archeology that are mentioned. An inexpensive bicycle odometer can be bought for about $20.00.

Out-and-Back versus Car Spotting

The description and length of each bike trail in this guide is for *one way* only. It is assumed that you will park your car at the beginning of the trail and ride "out and back." The author, who is not by any stretch of the imagination a bike pro, was able to ride every trail in this book out and back. You may prefer, however, to spot cars (parking one at each end of the trail). It is your choice. **Just remember to double the mileage if you are riding out and back.**

Equipment and Safety

The following information will allow you to make many enjoyable trips on the *Great Rail-Trails of the Northeast*. Proper equipment and safety practices can make the difference between a pleasant experience and a disappointing one. To ride the non-asphalt trails in this book you will need a Mountain Bike. Such bikes are relatively new on the market and are best recognized by their "fat" tires. The width of the tires prevents the bike from sinking into the sand or dirt found on some of the trails. Another common feature of these bikes is the greater number of gears compared to the old 10-speeds. This feature is welcome when you need an extremely low gear to go through sand or other soft surfaces. The very low gears will allow you to climb steep gradients with less difficulty. However, you will not encounter grades steeper than 2.5% on any of the trails in this book.

A cyclo-computer-odometer will make riding the *Great Rail-Trails of the Northeast* more enjoyable. Electronic odometers cost as low as $20.00 and are a valuable addition to any bike. Do not use a mechanical type as they are prone to failure and are not very accurate. The electronic types have a re-setable trip-odometer, clock and mile-per-hour functions. More expensive models indicate cadence, elapsed time, pulse rate monitor, kilometers, etc. The sky's the limit. You must, however, set them properly to match your tire size. Slight variations may introduce different odometer readings than those indicated in the trail descriptions. Take this into account when using this book.

Smiling bicyclist going past a trailside bike shop along
the Minuteman Trail in Arlington, Massachusetts

Your bike should also have a rack to hold panniers or other type of packs. Rain-gear should be one of the first items into the pack. A handle bar pack is a useful addition to hold maps (or this guide) and other readily needed materials. Never wear back packs while biking as they will raise your center of gravity and make for an unstable ride. A water bottle that mounts on the frame of the bike is a necessity also. To get to the trails means that you'll be transporting the bike with your car. Do not waste money on a cheap, unknown brand of bike rack. The best money you can spend will be on the highest quality rack you can obtain for your specific vehicle. Do not skimp here. You do not want to be losing your bike off the roof or trunk while on the highway.

Safety

The foremost concern while on a bicycle should be safety. When arriving at any trail-head you should first look for any signage that has to do with safety on that trail. Sometimes there is a different way of doing things on that trail that may be new to you or others in your party. Here are a few rules that apply to all trails.

(1) Wear a helmet. Broken bones and torn muscles will heal but a broken head will not.

(2) Wear bright colors. This is particularly important where vehicles may be encountered. Plan to be seen.

(3) Make sure your bike is in proper working order, especially the brakes.

(4) Invest in a rearview mirror, either the type that mounts on the handle-bar or the kind that mounts on the helmet.

(5) Ride on the right, and sound a horn or call out when passing.

(6) Ride responsibly with confidence and within your capabilities. Do not ride beyond your endurance, and if you ride alone, let someone know your itinerary.

(7) Carry a small tool kit and know how to use it to do minor, on-site repairs.

Great Rail-Trails of the Northeast

The main reason that the Airline South trail does not continue all the way to Willimantic: This bridge is over the Willimantic River, just west of the New Haven yard and the junction with the Midland Division, which today is known as the Hop River State Park Trail.

Great Rail-Trails of Connecticut

1. Airline State Park
2. Farmington Canal Park
3. Farmington Valley Greenway
4. Hop River Trail State Park
5. Larkin State Bridle Trail
6. Stratton Brook State Park

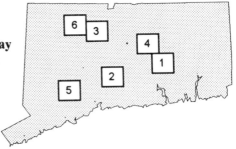

Connecticut is fortunate among the neighboring states in its inventory of rail-trails. A good population base of active enthusiasts, and an abundant supply of current and potential rail-trails means that Connecticut will be in the forefront of the Rails-to-Trails Movement.

The ongoing development of Willimantic, in eastern Connecticut, as a rail-trail mecca of sorts, bears watching. Here the Eastern Connecticut Chapter of the *National Railroad Historical Society* (NRHS) is rehabilitating the old New Haven Railroad yard just north of Bridge Street. This project involves the restoration of track, roundtable, rolling stock, and assorted railroad structures, and is at the center of three interesting trails that terminate here: Airline South, the Hop River Trail, and Airline North (a detailed guide of Airline North, will appear in the next edition of this book.). The positive spin-offs of the rail-trails in this area could be an economic boom and civic pride.

The Larkin State Bridle Trail is innovative in its primary dedication to equestrians. This trail is also special for the many fills that provide a different perspective to the view of the New England forest. Farmington Canal Park is a lovely ride through time to the days of the canal barge and that mode of transportation.

Farmington Valley Greenway provides a glimpse into the historic and quaint towns that lie just west of Hartford, and how the railroad affected them. The Farmington Valley Trails Council is a grass-roots organization working to expand the net-work there to over seventy safe miles of paths.

The Great Rail-Trails of Connecticut can provide a new angle on this interesting and hospitable state.

1 Airline South State Park Trail

Endpoints: Depot Hill Road, East Hampton, Connecticut to Bull Hill Road, Marlborough, Connecticut.
Location: Hartford County, towns of East Hampton and Marlborough, CT
Length: 7.3 miles
Surface: Gravel and original ballast

Uses:

To get there: Out of Middletown, Connecticut, follow CT 17/66 east through Portland. Stay on 66 until the intersection of 66 & 151. Take left here onto Depot Hill Road, go uphill approximately 1/2 mile. The place to park is where the transmission lines cross the road. Don't block the gate. Head east ,which is to the right as you drive up the hill.

Contact:
Joe Hickey, Bureau of Outdoor Recreation
Department of Environmental Protection
165 Capital Avenue, Hartford, Connecticut 06106
203-566-2304

John Hankins, Chairman
Windham Parks and Recreation Advisory Committee
203-423-9798 (home); 203-646-2469 (work)

Local resources for bike repairs/rentals:
Rainbow Cycle, 385 Valley Street., Willimantic, CT, 203-423-7182
Scott's Cyclery, 1171 Main Street, Willimantic, CT, 203-423-8889

The New York and Boston Railroad Company, nick-named the Airline, was dreamed up by Charles Alsop of Middletown, Connecticut. The main premise was to run passenger trains at great speed between New York and Boston. What made this plan different was the routing. This new route was 25 miles shorter and 1-1/2 hours faster than the Shoreline route. Starting in New Haven, Alsop began laying track to the northeast corner of Connecticut. Financial obstacles blocked the plan of Mr. Alsop and the project was reorganized to become the Boston & New York Airline Railroad. Now run by a Mr. Lyman, they proceeded to finish the line.

The first major geographic obstacle encountered was the Connecticut River at Middletown. The river is navigable in this section, so a swinging drawbridge was constructed here to allow marine traffic to pass by. Another major obstacle was the rolling ridges of east-central Connecticut. These were overcome by a straight ahead approach, making massive cuts through hills and long bridges over the valleys. The bridges in East Hampton, Connecticut were among the longest of their type in New England. They were known to sway under the weight of trains and many an engineer got gray hair on these crossings.

The "Rapallo," a bridge named for a director of the company, was 1,380 feet long and 60 feet high. The "Lyman," named for the first president of the railroad, was 1,100 feet long and about 150 feet above Dickinson Brook. These structures were considered marvels of modern engineering when built in 1873. They became obsolete within a few years, however, with the heavier weights of newer trains. The New Haven Railroad, the last railroad to own these bridges, filled them to the top with gravel in 1913. These immense monuments from an era long gone are still here -- just buried. Another claim to fame for this line was the special passenger train that was jointly run with the New York and New England Railroad. Known as the "Ghost Train" or the "White Train," it was the steam era's equivalent to the jet age's Concorde. Painted white to stress cleanliness and speed, these trains were the fashionable way to travel between Boston and New York. The late 19th-century American society elite (such as President Benjamin Harrison and author Rudyard Kipling) were passengers.

You are about to embark on the original route of the rich and famous.

New Haven Railroad - Old Airline depot, 1904
[courtesy of Richard Symmes, Walker Transportation Collection of the Beverly Historical Society]

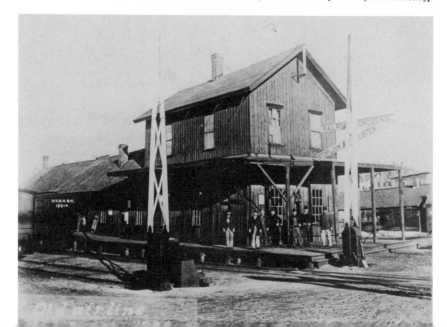

1. Airline State Park

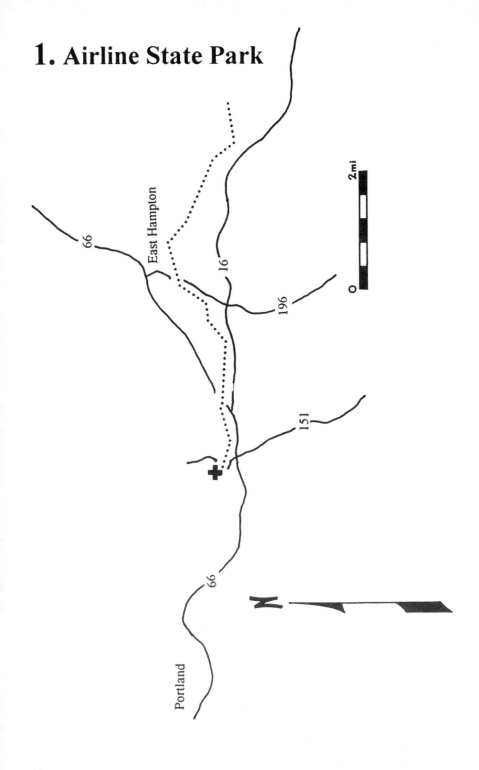

0.2 miles: The early going will be somewhat rocky because the power company maintains the right of way for access to their towers.

0.4 miles: Look closely and you'll see a cut that was allowed to fill-in and the path is now off to the side.

0.5 miles: Curving fill is located here. Impressive at 50 feet, it is only a hint of the big ones to come.

0.7 miles: Here is a big cut, known as Bishop's Cut, one of the largest in Connecticut. In this area there is a stream that runs along the trail for a while. This stream is here because the drainage ditches on each side of the road bed have filled with sediment over the years. Though a bit of a nuisance, the stream is not a great impediment. It is clean-running, not mucky and is only a couple of inches deep at the most.

0.9 miles: The trail has a fork here. The right branch will lead to Route 66, the last 50 feet being up a steep embankment. The straight branch will lead to a culvert/tunnel under the highway. The culvert has a sidewalk on the right side to get through the water more easily.

1.0 miles: The stream is now off to the side, and there are some remnants of Airline ballast and a stray tie or two for good measure.

1.6 miles: Grade crossing at Alden's Crossing, a residential street that is off of Route 16. Interestingly, the rail is still in place here at the crossing, even after all these years.

1.7 miles: Stone abutments here for a little bridge that is now gone. This is a wide gap of about a 20 feet. You have two choices; one is to go into the nearby and paralleling Route 16 or go down the embankment and ford the stream which is very shallow.

2.0 miles: Here the trail widens up and smooths out.

2.1 miles: Back on the ballast.

2.2 miles: Cut in this area has a stone wall in place to help hold the bank up. This is about .2 mile long.

2.4 miles: A fill is here which is about 25 feet high.

2.5 miles: The fill is getting taller now, over 70 feet high.

2.6 miles: The fill is gone and now a cut is becoming apparent. Expect some water in this cut, along with some junk including a 62 Rambler Station Wagon.

3.0 miles: Grade crossing at Forrest Road, then going past an old rail-served building that is today known as Lyon and Billard Lumber Company.

3.3 miles: You are now approaching the old Depot of East Hampton. It shows signs of recent repair and seems to have someone caring for it. Also in the general area are signs that a small yard and coaling facilities were once here. In this section you will have to go onto city streets for a short while, so be careful of cars. On the left you'll notice the Fire Station and it's parking lot. Go through here and take a right onto Route 196. East Hampton has a restaurant or two if you need a snack, and it is filled with antique stores to hunt around in. The town calls itself the "Bell-town of America" and has plenty of old mills to explore (some restored).

As you get underway again, you now have a decision to make.

(1) You can go down the street and turn left into a parking lot which has a large "Business Locator" Map on the street side. Go through the parking lot, up the embankment and back onto the rail-trail. There is a bridge straight ahead that goes over a small river. This bridge is a deck-girder type, but doesn't have a good surface to walk on. The original deck ties are still in-place and are somewhat rotted. Even if you have no intention of traversing this bridge, you should have a look anyway because the bridge was planned for two tracks, though only one was laid.

(2) The way around this obstruction is to continue down Route 196 and then take a left onto Walnut Avenue. This will rejoin the trail.

3.6 miles: Grade crossing of Walnut Avenue. Here also is located a small industry that at one time was rail served.

3.9 miles: Fill here which is about 30 feet high.

4.0 miles: Small pond and interesting colonial house are here.

4.1 miles: Grade crossing at Smith Street. Note the photogenic pond on the other side. Parking here also for trail users.

4.3 miles: Into the woods again with the original ballast to make it an interesting ride.

4.4 miles: Wide fill here as we go down-grade.

Admiring the view from the top of the Lyman Viaduct

26

4.9 miles: Big rock here which is about 35 feet high.

5.1 miles: The cut has leveled out now.

5.4 miles: Another cut has appeared.

5.5-5.8 miles: This is the Rapallo Viaduct. At 1380 feet long, this fill and its twin, the Lyman Viaduct, are the largest such areas in New England. If you look closely, you'll notice the steel in the ground along the way. This is the top of the bridge that spans this valley. The bridge is still here, under the gravel. The New Haven Railroad filled in the bridge in 1913, when the weight of the trains grew beyond the rating of the structure. When the New Haven was switching from steam to diesel power (from 1949-1952), they ran a regular excursion over this route. The scenic beauty found on the two viaducts is a part of forgotten New England. It is an understatement to say that this is a good place to rest and take in the view.

5.9 miles: Into a cut here that stands about 20 feet tall. This one is dry.

6.0 miles: Small fill here with a horse farm and meadow beyond the tree line.

6.2 miles: Here the ground on the right drops away and the left side has a hill that climbs above you and then drops to your level.

6.3 miles: Another cut, a dry one again and not too large.

6.4 miles: Fill here is about 50 feet above the surrounding forest.

6.6 miles: Fill continues and the floor of the forest drops away, now 90 feet below.

6.7 miles: Small cut here.

6.9-7.1 miles: Here you'll find the Lyman Viaduct, the grand-daddy of filled bridges in New England. A little more than 1100 feet long and nearly 150 feet in height, this will take your breath away. This structure and the Rapallo were designed to have twin tracks so they are plenty wide at the top to accommodate the people that show up for the views. Sightseers bring a picnic lunch and watch the hawks ride the thermals through the surrounding valleys.

7.2 miles: Remains of a telegraph pole and a meadow on the left that is being developed into a Christmas tree farm. Here also is a small cut.

7.3 miles: Grade crossing for Bull Hill Road. Parking is available here for the tourists that have come to view the viaducts. This is the effective end of the trail as there are large rivers ahead and the bridges are no longer in place. In the future the state plans to finish the trail to the terminus in Willimantic.

2 Farmington Canal Linear Park

Endpoints: Lock 12 Park, Cheshire, Connecticut, to Hamden, Connecticut.
Location: New Haven County, towns of Cheshire and Hamden, Connecticut.
Length: 2.8 miles paved. 5.2 miles total.
Surface: Asphalt and gravel

Uses:

To get there: Follow Rte 84 to Exit 26. Follow Rte 70 east towards Cheshire; and at junction with Rte 10, take Rte 10 south. At junction with Rte 42 west, follow Rte 42 past church and school. Lock 12 Park is on the left, with plenty of parking.

Contact:
Bob Ceccolini
Cheshire Department of Parks and Recreation
559 South Main Street
Cheshire, CT 06410
203-672-2743

Hamden Department of Parks and Recreation
203-287-2579

Local resources for bike repairs/rentals:
Alpine Ski Works, 209 W. Main Street, Cheshire, 203-272-6614
The Bike Rack, 2348 Whitney Avenue, Hamden, 203-288-7878.

In the mid 1820s, before there were any railroads, the most economical way to move freight was by water. Inland, that meant a canal. The bustling city of New Haven had business interests that financed a canal that started at the New Haven Harbor and went through the towns of Hamden, Cheshire, Southington, Plainville, Farmington, Avon, Simsbury, and Granby, Connecticut, all the way to Northampton Massachusetts, and beyond the natural falls at Enfield and Holyoke.

Running a distance of 83 miles, it was the longest canal in New England. It opened after only six years of construction, and in 1828, it was the engineering marvel of its time. The Farmington Canal was surpassed only by the Erie Canal in New York (in terms of length).

It was 36 feet wide at the surface and had a depth of 4 feet. The canal was made possible by the inclusion of over 25 locks and an aqueduct over the Farmington River, all constructed without modern equipment, and using only men, oxen, shovels, and picks. The canal was operational until the railroad was built in 1848, when the canal was then abandoned. The railroad was owned by the New Haven Railroad, until it was spun-off onto Penn-Central and then Conrail. The rail line was in daily use until 1982 when a flood caused a washout in Cheshire. The State of Connecticut took over the unwanted section at about this time, and a rail-trail was eventually created.

This lovely park is an important reminder of the two kinds of transportation prevalent in days gone by, and yet today, it continues to serve as a part of a modern "transportation system," the information super-highway, with its buried fiber-optic cable. The irony is overlooked by most people. The stretch of active rail north of the trail was recently operated by the Springfield Terminal Railroad operating unit of Guilford Transportation Industries (GTI). In early 1995, GTI petitioned the ICC and the State of Connecticut with the intention of abandoning the section of track to Southington. This would effectively cut off the last two customers in the area.

Though somewhat in the center of the trail, Lock 12 Park is the best place to start. Heading North, and crossing North Brooksvale Road, we begin.

Roller-blader on the trail in Cheshire, Connecticut.

2. Farmington Canal Park

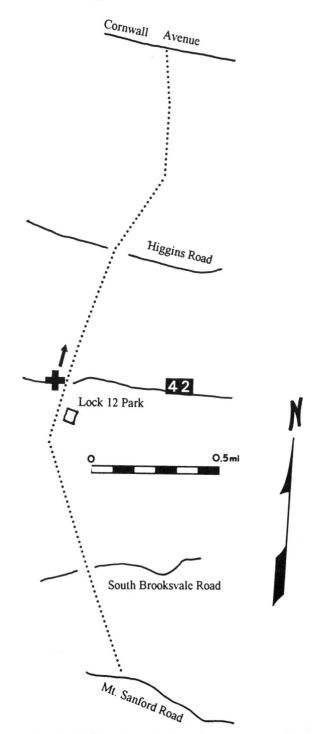

Cornwall Avenue

Higgins Road

42

Lock 12 Park

0   0.5 mi

N

South Brooksvale Road

Mt. Sanford Road

0.2 miles: It is already apparent here that this will be a trail with varied and plentiful flora, especially the type found along streams.

0.3 miles: We now pass over a wooden bridge of modern construction designed to look rustic. Built with pressure-treated timbers, it is made to last.

0.5 miles: At about this point the canal becomes closer, and though only approximately 12 feet wide here, it is clear that this was once a canal.

0.6 miles: Grade crossing over Higgins Road. This has been arranged in a nice way with inlaid brick or tile to give an audible warning to the users of the trail in addition to the normal visual warnings of signs and painted lines.

0.7 miles: The canal now widens to about 25-30 feet and has ducks (and sometimes swans) in residence. Look for the great abundance of clover flowering in mid-June. A dazzling display.

1.4 miles: Crossing over another wooden bridge, you approach a suburban neighborhood with lawns bordering the canal.

1.5 miles: The improved trail ends here, but on the other side of Cornwall Avenue it is apparent that the railroad is still in place and continues to serve local industry, such as Dolphin Enterprises, which supplies the area's building contractors. This is the area that is subject to the abandonment proceedings.

Going back to the parking lot and heading in the other direction: (Re-set your odometer)

0.1 miles: Another wooden bridge can be found here as you cross a feeder into the canal. Looking underneath, you can find the old stone foundation common to New Haven designs of the late nineteenth century. You are also coming upon the Park's namesake.

Lock Number 12. This historic area contains a rebuilt lock of the early nineteenth century. A lock was a device to raise or lower a canal boat to get over hills. It was actually a simple operation. When the pilot or master approached the lock, the lock master would open the wall in front of the boat. Next he would close and seal it. Water would then be pumped into or drained out, depending on the direction of travel. When the level reached the same height as the adjoining area, the other wall would be opened, and the boat would be on its way. This system is still in use today on the Panama Canal.

At the end of this complex, the trail crosses over the canal via a beautiful stone arch bridge that is similar to some of the New Haven's other arched bridges. One that comes right to mind, is the bridge over the Farmington River at Windsor Connecticut, which is still used daily by Conrail, GTI and Amtrak. This one is smaller, but is very picturesque next to the old buildings nearby. Looking into the canal below the bridge, you will see turtles. In the spring, Wood Ducks are known to nest here.

The namesake locks at Lock 12 Park.

0.4 miles: The canal is particularly lovely here, and has a sandy area for cooling your feet, if you are so inclined.

0.8 miles: South Brooksvale Road crosses here.

1.1 miles: Another wooden bridge.

1.3 miles: Grade crossing at Mt. Sanford Road and the south end of the paved trail. This is the Hamden/Cheshire line. The trail continues, however, as an unimproved one with gravel and sand as the base. In 1995, it will be improved as a paved trail.

1.5 miles: As of 1994, this part of the trail grows more primitive, and the path is fairly narrow. Plan to be alert because there are low-hanging branches. The canal is now on the left as you move south and is not in good shape at all. There is not much water; it is little more than a swampy ditch with aquatic plants abounding. MCI has laid cable in the bed of the canal.

1.6 miles: The trail start to rise on a fill, and is separated from the canal by a retaining wall.

1.7 miles: Here is a grave yard for ties pulled out but not properly disposed of.

1.8 miles: The trail crosses over the canal again at this point. The railroad used a deck-girder bridge, which is still in place but not easily traversed by bike. The preferred path is down to the right and back up onto the trail.

2.2 miles: Power lines cross the trail overhead.

2.4 miles: A small, derelict bridge crosses the canal here and leads to a parallel street.

2.5 miles: A Christmas Tree farm is found now on the left, and also some of the original rail. Left behind by the scrappers, it is sitting off to the side and seems to be of the fairly light variety.

2.6 miles: A small deck-girder bridge is here, followed by a grade crossing. The grade crossing is a challenge because the state of Connecticut blocked the road by means of a guard rail that goes into the brush on both sides of the trail, forcing you to lift your bike over and then climb over yourself. Not insurmountable, but definitely not user-friendly. Should be up-graded in 1995.

2.9 miles: An interesting piece of rail archeology can be seen here at this grade crossing. Note the timbers set into the street next to the rails. This is rarely seen in 1990s New England

3.1 miles: Another grade crossing with timbers. A golf course is visible here, off to the left, and across Rte 10, which is now close by and parallel.

3.2 miles: With land-taking by abutters, you are now forced to go into the canal bed, which is dry but very sandy and not fun to ride at all. After about 200 yards you can go back onto the main trail. Interesting ground covers can be seen in the shady areas here. You do have a choice, however. Rather than going into the canal, if you go into the street and follow Rte 10 south about 200 yards, you can easily rejoin the trail.

3.7 miles: Grade Crossing again.

3.8 miles: The trail now comes upon a stream about 20 feet down an embankment with no signs of a rail bridge. The increasing difficulty of following the trail will force you to turn back. In the construction season of 1995, this area in Hamden will be up-graded to a more pleasant experience.

3 Farmington Valley Greenway

End points: Currently within the town of Simsbury, Connecticut at Drake Hill Road and the Intersection of Rtes 202 and 315. However, the master plan calls for the eventual inclusion of others towns within a few years.
Location: Hartford County, Simsbury, Connecticut
Length: 2.2 miles
Surface: Asphalt and a parallel dirt/gravel path.

Uses:

To get there: Follow Route 10/202 into Simsbury. Just north of the intersection with Route 167/309, head east onto Drake Hill Road. Go about .2 mile and turn right onto Old Bridge Road. Park where it is wide at the foot of the old bridge over the Farmington River.
Contact:
Gerard G. Toner, Director
Department of Culture, Parks and Recreation
933 Hopmeadow Street
Simsbury, CT 06070
203-651-3751

Preston Reed, President
Farmington Valley Trail Council
5 Maple Street, Farmington, CT 06032
203-677-0611

Local resources for bike repairs/rentals:
Bicycle Cellar, 532 Hopmeadow Street, Simsbury, 203-658-1311.
Farmington Bicycle Shop, Post Office Sq., Farmington, 203-677-2453.
Neckers, 1591 Hopmeadow Street, Simsbury, 203-658-5783.

A coalition of Farmington Valley communities, with the support of Farmington Valley Trails Council, is spearheading the construction of a multi-town trail using the rights-of-way of both the Central New England Railroad and the New Haven Railroad's Canal Branch. When complete, the regional trail system will consist of a 25-mile multi-use trail through the towns of Suffield, East Granby, Simsbury, Avon, and Farmington. A second connection will be made to reach the old rail-beds in the towns of Plainville, Unionville, Collinsville, Burlington and Canton, adding 16 miles. A five-year plan is in place and on schedule with a completion in the year 1999 as the goal.

A similar multi-town project is just getting underway in Massachusetts. This would connect these ex-NH Canal Branch, Connecticut projects, with the towns of Southwick, Westfield, Southampton, Easthampton, and finally end at Northampton where the present City Bikeway (ex-NH Williamsburg Branch) and the Norwottuck (ex-B&M, Central Mass Division) are presently enjoyed by thousands of users each month.

When completed, the Farmington Valley trail system components will be the Farmington River Trail (16 miles long) and the Farmington Valley Greenway (22 miles long). These will be combined with the Farmington Canal Heritage Trail which will produce a trail with a total length of about 88 miles.

The section you are about to begin was paved in the late fall of 1994. The construction season of 1995 will see the extension south completed.

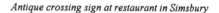

Antique crossing sign at restaurant in Simsbury

3. Farmington Valley Greenway

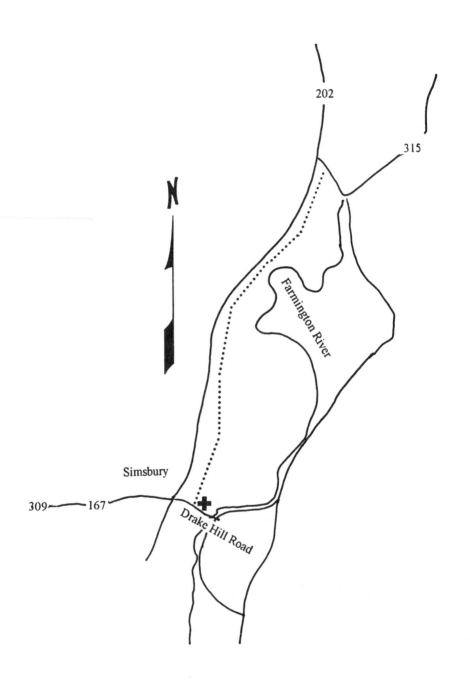

0.0 miles: Start out by going back up Drake Hill Road and turn right onto Iron Horse Blvd. The trail will be the sidewalk along the street for a while.

0.2 miles: Mall Way is on the left. Take a detour to see the old Simsbury Passenger Station that is now converted to offices. Along here the NH served a variety of businesses. The Hardware Store, next to the passenger depot, used to receive products by rail. A little further beyond is a restored NH freight transfer station that has been restored and converted to a restaurant. This place has much in the way of railroad memorabilia, including a NH caboose and a cosmetically restored narrow-gauge steam engine.

0.3 miles: Back onto the trail and continuing to head north, you will come upon the Town of Simsbury's Greenway area. This is a series of paths through the adjoining forested parcel.

0.6 miles: Driveway to a business that stores trailers; across the street is Andy's Center Shops.

0.9 miles: Driveway access to Simscroft Farms General Contractor's facility. Look out for approaching dump trucks.

1.1 miles: Here the trail diverges from Iron Horse Blvd. by going straight north, while the road turns west to join with Rte 10/202. The trail in this newly paved area is about 10 feet wide and has an adjacent dirt path that is appropriate for joggers.

1.3 miles: Slight cut as you go uphill.

1.4 miles: Route 10/202 is directly to the left and about 20 feet above you. The Farmington River is getting near on the right.

1.6 miles: The highway is now at the same level as the trail.

1.7 miles: The river has meandered away from you and all that is nearby there is the flood plain. An interesting retaining wall is here. Built of 6"x 8" concrete ties, all interlocked, this type is not seen that often anymore.

2.2 miles: The finished trail ends at the intersection of Rtes. 315 & 10/202.

Bicyclist on the Hop River Trail in winter

4 Hop River State Park Trail

Endpoints: *Option A:* Steel Crossing Road, Bolton, Connecticut, passing through Andover, Coventry, and Columbia and ending at Route 66 in Willimantic, Connecticut.
   Option B: Church Street, Vernon, Connecticut, and continues onto Steel Road Crossing, as above.
Location: Tolland, and Windham Counties, Connecticut.
Length: *Option A:* 12.0 miles
   Option B: 18.8 miles
Surface: Gravel and a small amount of original ballast

Uses:

To get there: *Option A:* Take I-384 east to Route 6. Steel Crossing Road will be the fourth right. The trail bisects the road on top of the hill, about .2 mile from the highway.
   Option B: Take exit 64-65 off of I-84, then follow Rte 30 north for a short distance and take right turn onto Dobson Road. Go past Dobsonville Pond on left and take left onto Church Street. Park where it is safe or otherwise permitted on the left. This is the start of the trail. Head east, which is the direction you took onto Church Street.

Contact:
Joe Hickey
Bureau of Outdoor Recreation
Department of Environmental Protection
165 Capital Avenue, Hartford, Connecticut 06106
1-203-566-2304

John Hankins, Chairman
Windham Parks & Recreation Advisory Committee.
1-203-423 9798 (home)
1-203-646-2469 (work)

Local resources for bike repairs/rentals:
Cycle Center, Rt. 30 Post Road Plaza, Vernon, 203-872-7740
The Bike Shop, 681 Main Street, Manchester, 203-647-1027
Rainbow Cycle, 385 Valley Street, Willimantic, 203-423-7182
Scott's Cyclery, 1171 Main Street, Willimantic, 203-423-8889

One of the earliest railroads to be chartered in New England was the Manchester Railroad Company in 1833. This was built to move the stone quarried at Bolton to Hartford, where the Connecticut River provided access to distant markets. After the usual round of mergers and acquisitions, this line became known as The Hartford, Providence and Fishkill Railroad. The line was laid east to Providence, Rhode Island, and as far west as Waterbury, Connecticut, when the money for development ran out. The company then was merged into The New York and New England Railroad, which then proceeded to complete the extension to Beacon, N.Y. in 1882, where a car ferry transferred freight over the Hudson River. The cost of this work weakened the NY & NE to the point where the all powerful New Haven Railroad took over in 1891.

This railroad carried 30 to 40 trains a day in the late 19th century. Every year, hundreds of thousands of passengers went over the "Notch" at Bolton, to Willimantic, and then to points beyond. Willimantic, Connecticut, was the rail mecca of New England around the turn of the century. Scores of passenger trains arrived daily. Two divisions of the New Haven Railroad and the Central Vermont Railway (now New England Central), had yard facilities in this city that stretched over a mile long.

As the automobile came into popularity, the vast network of branches became superfluous to the New Haven, and passenger service ended between Manchester and Willimantic in 1933. The line had diminishing levels of freight traffic until the takeover of the New Haven by the Penn-Central Railroad in 1968. Penn Central was not interested in developing any traffic on this line, and proceeded to formally abandon the line in 1970. The State of Connecticut has since acquired the right-of-way as a rail-trail and named it the Hop River Trail State Park, after the river that parallels it for much of the journey. The route from Bolton Notch to Willimantic is a portion of the Charter Oak Greenway, which is a state-sponsored bike path that is part of the East Coast Greenway, which will eventually run from Boston, to Washington, DC.

There are two ways to ride this trail. *Option A* is a shorter version that avoids muddy and sometimes deep water. *Option B* covers the whole trail.

This trail does have some challenging areas because some of the bridges have less-than-desirable decks. Sometimes this means bridges with no decks except girders about 18" wide to walk on. (This is not as difficult as it sounds because there are multiple girders next to one another.) In some situations, there are bridges with the timber ties still in place, which means you'll have a stepping-stone type walk across the bridge. In other places the bridges are out entirely. In these cases, an alternative, easy way around the bridge is indicated in the guide.

4 B Hop River Trail State Park

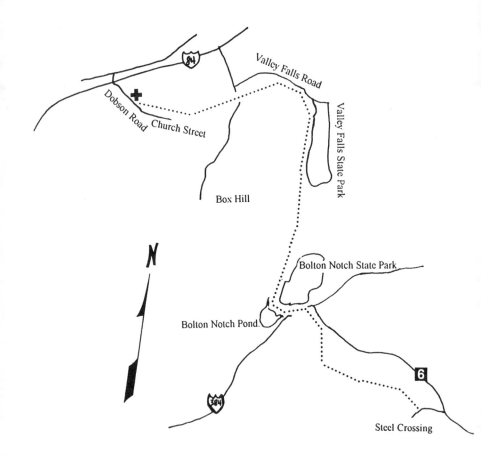

Option B: **Starting point** Church St., in the Dobsonville section of Vernon CT.

0.0 miles: This area will be undergoing significant improvement by the town of Vernon in the construction season of 1995. A stone-dust surface will be installed at that time.
0.2 miles: There used to be a bridge that was in place here to cross Phoenix Street. It is no longer installed, but instead can be seen on the west side of the approach. It may be reinstalled at a later date. Be careful crossing over the other side because it is a blind approach for cars.
0.9 miles: This is the start of a fill on the approach to a street known as Tunnel Road.
1.1 miles: Here is the towering fill over Tunnel Road. You are now about 40 feet above the roadway. Note the cars passing through the tunnel with alternating traffic flow, due to the bore being only wide enough for one lane of traffic. It is a local tradition of courtesy to have one car pass north and then one car pass south. No one breaks the rules.
1.2 miles: Here is an abandoned building off the right. This may have had a railroad purpose. The construction of the walls seem to be much more substantial than what would be found in residential buildings.
1.7 miles: As you notice the trail starting to swing to the right (south), you are in the area of Valley Falls State Park. Valley Falls Road is on the left about 70 feet below you. The lay of the land here is what you will typically see for a while: high hills with numerous outcroppings of rock on the right, and a valley of various depths on the left. Shenipsit Trail (blue blazes) enters the rail-trail from the left and runs along with you for about a mile.
2.2 miles: Down in the valley to the left is the pond at Valley Falls Park.
3.2 miles: The tall hill to the right is known as Box Hill, which is about 200 feet higher than the trail. Note the abundant mountain. laurel in the area. Geologist, John Hankins, has pointed out that the outcrops on the right are composed of a metamorphic rock called garnet staurolite schist. Examine the rocks that have broken off the cliff for small red garnets and rectangular staurolite crystals.
3.6 miles: In this area is a pavilion for Bolton Notch State Park. It is located on the left, just off the trail. Notice that the path was wide enough for double track. At one time this area had a passing siding to allow trains to pass one another.
4.2 miles: Here you'll find an unusual bridge which allows Railroad Brook to cross the trail and is made of rail. Many pieces are laid in place and sitting on top of a concrete constructed abutment.
4.3 miles: Grade crossing of a dirt road that is actually a long driveway for the one lonely house that is nearby. Just after the crossing is a deep cut. This is usually wet and a detour can be found by following the dirt road that is parallel to the rail-bed. It will rejoin the trail in about .2 mile. The trail swings to the left here to get under Rte 6 by way of a tunnel.

4.4 miles: The pond on the right is called Bolton Notch Pond. The long uphill grade is about to crest and change to downhill.

4.6 miles: You are now at the approach to the tunnel under the I-384/Rte 6 interchange area. It is likely to be very wet here on each side of the tunnel. The tunnel itself dates back to 1951, is about 250 feet long and is built of reinforced concrete. Of course it is filled with graffiti. The water that is spring-fed and pours down on the approaches, turns into huge columns of ice in the winter. You can find ice climbers here in the winter! Stay and watch them challenge the wall. The summer brings a cool mist to the area.

4.7 miles: As you exit the tunnel, you will be in a deep cut, over 30 feet in height. Rte 6 is on the left and will be your companion for the rest of the way to Willimantic.

5.2 miles: The trail turns right (south) for a bit as Rte 6 takes a steep downhill grade. It is in this area that the Bolton Ice Palace is found. A fill with a broad top carries the rail-trail on a shallower downhill grade. The fill is very wide, suggesting that this area was once the site of double trackage.

5.6 miles: On the left a small pond may be visible through the trees. This is Johnson Pond, part of a Boy Scout Camp.

6.8 miles: Grade crossing at Steel Crossing Road.

Option A: **Starting point.** Steel Crossing Road. Those continuing from *Option B* should re-set their odometers back to 0.0 now.

0.0 miles: The first notable feature is a small rock cut. This initial area has the original ballast still in place.

0.1 miles: Cut-stone culvert under the trail carries water from the hill on the right.

0.2 miles: Wash-board effect is evident here.

0.4 miles: Occasional ties can be found here, along with a fill.

0.6 miles: The valley and Route 6 are about 100 feet below as we continue to hug the side of the mountain.

0.7 miles: Here can be seen a fairly big (50 feet) rock cut as the trail curves to the right and you head towards Willimantic. Moss grows on one side of the cut.

0.9 miles: A bit of a fill is here as you come into some more of the washboard effect.

1.2 miles: Grade crossing at Bailey Road. The road actually ends before the trail but a residential driveway is the continuation. Also in this sector is the Andover border.

1.3 miles: Boulders are here to prevent cars from entering the trail. Here also are some reminders of the past, telegraph poles with four cross-arms, but without wires. This is a sure sign that at one time this line was a busy place. There is also a small rock cut here with the original ballast still in place.

4 A Hop River State Park Trail

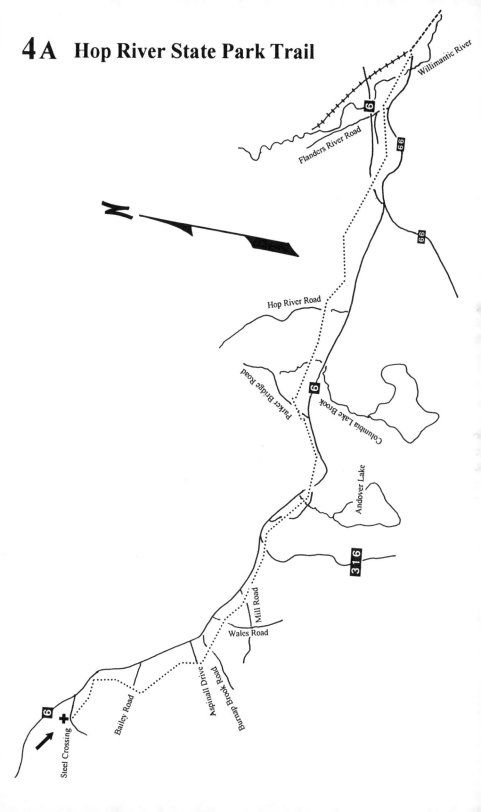

Derelict telegraph pole with multiple cross-arms,
evidence that this area was once bursting with traffic.

1.5 miles: A whistle marker here, which originally warned of the crossing we just passed. The cross-arms on the derelict telegraph poles have increased to five arms now. The fill in this area is fairly substantial at 20 feet on the right and 40 feet on the left.

1.6 miles: Deck-girder bridge here. This one is different from most rail bridges, in that the girders are not tall in height and strength, but eight girders have been placed in series to increase load carrying rating. At approximately 20 feet wide, this will not be a problem to cross because of the number of girders to walk on. A detour for those who prefer, is to go back to Bailey Road, down the hill to Rte 6, and then to Aspinall Drive.

1.7 miles: A large wooden obelisk is found here. All markings are obliterated, but it is likely this is a mile marker put in place by the old predecessor railroad

1.9 miles: A rail stand off to the right here marks a problem area for the railroad. There must have been washouts in this section necessitating the stockpiling of spare rails.

2.0 miles: Grade crossing at Aspinall Drive. An active shooting range is in this area and they do "turkey shoots" here most Sundays. Detouring via the road is recommended if you hear shooting.

2.3 miles: At certain times of the year, the rock cut in this area can be wet, but not too bad. Also here is another fill.

2.5 miles: Grade crossing here is Burnap Brook Road.

2.9 miles: Grade crossing at Wales Road.

3.3 miles: This area can be wet at certain times.

3.4 miles: Mill Road grade crossing.

3.5 miles: Route 6 is getting closer and some original ties are still in place here. As you enter the center of Andover, the trail runs immediately adjacent to Route 6 atop a five foot high retaining wall.

3.8 miles: A mile marker is here but no numbers can be made out.

3.9 miles: Route 6 is adjacent to us here and the trail goes through the parking lot of the Andover Custom Exhaust Company, which used to be a rail served industry of some sort years ago.

4.0 miles: At the back side of the auto shop and flush with the ground is the outline of the footing for the Andover passenger station. A switch is still here.

4.1 miles: On a fill here with Jasper's Convenience Store just below. This is a good place to rest and get a drink.

4.2 miles: Intersection of Route 6 and Route 316 is here. The railroad used to cross over Rte 316 via a bridge, but this is no longer here and the trail ends with barriers to prevent someone from sailing over the end to the road below. Fortunately, however, there is a way down the embankment and up the other side back onto the trail.

4.5 miles: A small rock cut is seen here. This area can be wet at times.

4.7 miles: This section has some ties still in place, but has enough room to maneuver on the side.

4.9 miles: Merritt Valley Road is here. A bridge used to be in place, but there is an easy way down and back.

5.0 miles: Bridge across a feeder stream from Andover Lake is ahead. This doesn't have a safe deck, but there is an outlet to parallel-running Merritt Valley Road. and back to the trail.

5.2 miles: On a fill again now as you come upon another open bridge. There is a pathway around this obstacle, so don't give-up.

5.3 miles: Residential neighborhood is here as you cross under Route 6. Look closely on each side of the bridge approaches and you'll see the old concrete footings for the tell-tale signals. They were used to warn the train men who might have been on the roofs of the cars, that a restricted clearance area was ahead ... time to duck! This device was not much more than a cross-arm over the tracks with a series of ropes or wires that hung off it and brushed against anything that was too tall.

5.7 miles: Ties are here as you cross over a big fill. In this general area is a concrete culvert over the Andover Lake Stream. The date "1912" is visible on the south side (upstream) of the culvert.

6.5 miles: Marsh is here on both sides of you.

6.8 miles Grade crossing at Parker Bridge Road as you enter into Columbia.

7.0 miles: This is an open area with a lot of cinder and coal droppings. This may have been a water stop for steam engines at one time.

7.2 miles: Big fill here with a wetlands down below that is the beginning of the namesake, Hop River.

7.4 miles: The water is still here and it becomes apparent that beaver activity is the reason for the elevated levels.

7.5 miles: A bridge across the Columbia Lake Brook. This is an open deck bridge about 20 feet long, but is crossable if you are careful. The 18"-girders provide the walkway and there are 4 to walk on. After the bridge you'll come upon original ballast again. A detour is to go back to Parker Bridge Road, then down Rte 6 to Hop River Road, and back onto the trail.

7.7 miles: You now come upon a swimming hole. This is just what you would imagine as a perfect spot, complete with a tarzan swing from a towering tree over the wide and slow running river.

7.8 miles: Another small bridge is here. This one is only 20 feet long and once again has an open deck.

Tunnel under I-384/Rte 6 area in Bolton Notch Connecticut.

8.0 miles: Here's a bridge over the Hop River. This one is about 150 feet in length and, as is usual on this trail, less than desirable. This time it is a deck-girder type, but most of the timber-ties are still in place. It is crossable.

8.2 miles: Grade crossing at Hop River Road. This is where the detour at the 7.5 mile mark rejoins the trail. This section is one of the best so far, in terms of the type of surface. Wide, hard surfaced, and smooth are words that come to mind here.

8.4 miles: On a fill again with the Hop River on the right. A meadow is on the left as we traverse the border between Coventry and Columbia.

8.9 miles: Access out to a meadow here.

9.3 miles: Here is evidence of some new "Rail-Trail" construction with a tunnel / culvert that was fabricated in 1990. This is Coventry Road overhead.

9.5 miles: You are now crossing the right-of-way of an underground high-pressure gas transmission line.

9.6 miles: On a fill again with a sand quarry on either side of you.

Culvert/Bridge in the Bolton area on the Hop River Trail.

10.0 miles: Here's an interesting bridge. Although only 6 feet wide, it is of an unusual construction. Rail is the material used here. Placed side-by-side, they formed the deck of the bridge.

10.1 miles: Route 6 Expressway passes overhead.

10.3 miles: Here's an old concrete mile marker but has no markings left on it. There is also a big fill in this area. Route 66 is visible off to the right.

10.4 miles: Washboard trail surface is here.

10.6 miles: Now into a small cut.

10.8 miles: Kings Road neighborhood is in this area with some back yards that abut the trail.

10.9 miles: Bridge across the Hop River again. This bridge has a collapsing abutment and it may not be advisable to cross until DEP obtains moneys to restore this structure. Kings Road to Flanders River Road will take you back on the trail.

11.2 miles: Flanders River Road is overhead as you are in another modern tunnel / culvert.

11.5 miles: This is the Willimantic border and Route 66 is right next to the trail in this area. Just ahead the ties and rail will still be in place and the New England Central Railroad's main-line will be joining up. At this point you can go down Rte 66 to Mackey's, a garden-home-center store, a short distance away. Here you can pick-up a single track trail that continues east along the Willimantic River. To find the trail, cross the river via the highway bridge and turn left into Mackey's. Take another left down a dirt road and pass under the highway to the head of the trail.

12.0 miles: Here, at the site of a trestle over the river, is the junction of the Airline South Trail (ex-Airline division of the New Haven Railroad), and the Hop River Trail, (ex-Midland Division of the New Haven Railroad). This area was once the New Haven's yard in Willimantic. Today the Eastern Connecticut Chapter of the National Railroad Historical Society is restoring parts of this facility for a museum and you may see some of the volunteers at work. They plan to incorporate the network of rail-trails that terminate in Willimantic into their vision of a tourist destination that will include a rest area, various ex-New Haven RR buildings moved to the site, and a tourist train (which they hope to run on the old Providence and Worcester Railroad trackage that is accessed about 1/2 mile south of the Bridge Street area). The single track trail continues eastward along the river a short distance, to downtown Willimantic where the 1995 construction season will see a finished path take shape that will lead to the Airline North Trail.

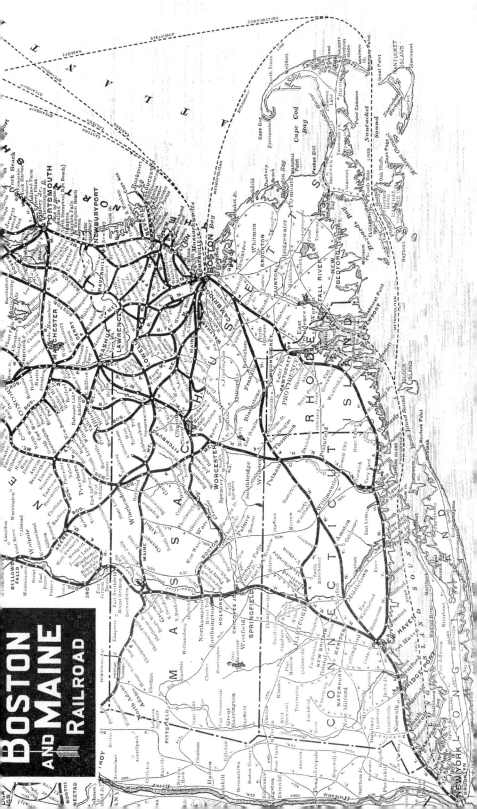

5 Larkin Bridle Trail

Endpoints: Southbury Fire Station, Southbury, Connecticut to Route 63 Waterbury, Connecticut.
Location: New Haven County, Connecticut. Passing through Southbury, Oxford, and Waterbury, Connecticut.
Length: 8.2 miles
Surface: Original ballast and cinders

Uses:

To get there: Take Route 84 past Waterbury; take Exit 16, Route 188 South. Follow this for about 1.5 miles and park just past the Southbury Fire Station on the left. Look for small brown rectangular sign marking the State Bridle Trail.
Contact:
Tim O'Donoghue, Supervisor, Southford Falls State Park
175 Quaker Farms Road, Route 188, Southbury, CT 06488 (203-264-5169)
Local resources for bike repairs/rentals:
The Bike Rack, 1059 Huntington Avenue, Waterbury, 203-755-0347.

Originally built in 1881 and owned by the New York and New England Railroad, this trail is the only one in Connecticut meant to be used primarily as a bridle path for horses. Traversing the beautiful rolling hills of western Connecticut, this line once boasted the only direct passenger service to eastern New York from Waterbury, CT. With hand tools and the strong backs of Irish immigrants, this railroad was constructed with some of the steepest grades in all of Connecticut, up to 3%. As you travel this trail, you'll notice that the fills are very long and high. Originally these areas were trestles, but were filled with cinders and other materials which reduced maintenance costs.

The New York and New England Railroad was taken over by the New Haven Railroad in 1891, and the line became known as the Western District of the Highland Division of the New Haven. With both passenger and freight service, including a milk train, this line was busy until the Depression. The formal abandonment with the Interstate Commerce Commission took place in 1937. This trail's primary use is equestrian. It was given to the state for this purpose, although non-motorized usage is not prohibited by deed restriction or other language. In order to preserve a safe environment for horses and their riders, a move is under-way to restrict biking speed and the number of bikes in a group. This is necessary because the top of the many elevated sections is narrow.

Photogenic Towantic Pond on the Larkin Bridle Trail.

0.1 miles: Here is a cedar tree growing in what must of been the right of way. It is of substantial height and diameter, and is not something you expect to see in the middle of a trail.

0.4 miles: This is the first of the big fills that you will be seeing. This one is at least forty feet high and about 2/10's of a mile long, with a pond along the side. In this area is an impressive stone arched bridge which crosses 8 Mile Brook.

0.7 miles: Grade crossing at Pope Road.

1.2 miles: Grade crossing at Hawley Road.

1.5 miles: Watching the trail carefully, you'll see some railroad ties. Still in their original places, they are probably approaching their 75th year.

1.7 miles: Another big fill over 40 feet high.

2.0 miles: Grade crossing at Christian Street. Due north of this road is the south end of Oxford Airport in Southbury, Connecticut.

2.8 miles: We now come upon a small rock cut, which in all probability was cut by hand.

3.0 miles: Crossing at Towantic Hill Road.

3.6 miles: Towantic Pond is to the right. Look for the abundant frog population basking on the lily pads.

5. Larkin State Bridle Trail

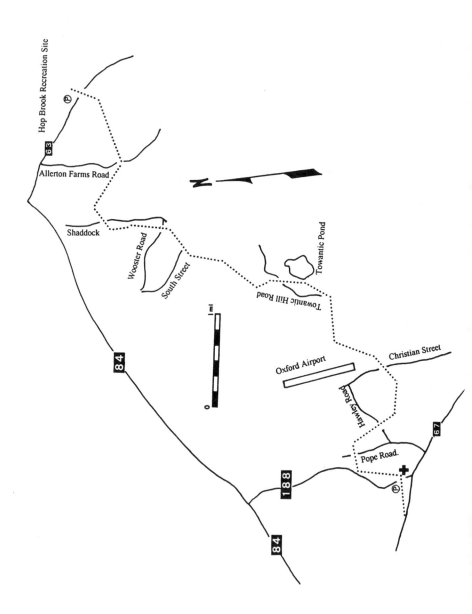

4.0 miles: This area is a private section and has "NO TRESPASSING" signs. It is strewn with numerous small felled trees. The ditch on the side has filled with sediment over the years, thus allowing water to flow across the trail. This section can be avoided by taking a right at the grade crossing and then your next left. You will shortly rejoin the trail. The town of Oxford has purchased this section for an industrial sewer line. After this construction is completed, this stretch should be improved in 1995.

4.2 miles: Another big fill which on the south side of the trail is 35 feet high and on the north side is 20 feet high.

4.4 miles: A brook passes under the fill with a falls on the south side.

4.6 miles: Grade crossing

4.7 miles: Another fill

5.3 miles: South Street crossing with the abutment of the original bridge nearby. It makes for an interesting scene.

5.6 miles: Another fill that is 25 feet high on the south side and 15 feet on the north side, and a grade crossing at Wooster Road.

5.8 miles: Rock cut through a small hill and then it becomes apparent that you are now on the side of a mountain. Steep drop-off to the right with Shaddock Road below. To the left is an uphill incline.

6.0 miles: You've entered a special place, a primitive rock-cut that is today filled in with a canopy of trees and ferns. It is probably 10-to-15 degrees cooler than the previous area. The cooler temperatures and humidity support the ferns and exotic ground covers.

6.3 miles: Another grade crossing.

6.8 miles: Grade crossing of a fire trail.

7.1 miles: Another big fill with a 50-foot drop to either side.

7.3 miles: Grade crossing at Allerton Farms Road. There used to be a bridge here so there is a great height difference. Be careful.

7.5 miles: Muddy, low-lying area.

7.6 miles: Beautiful lake with mansion on the shore and a fill approximately 30 feet high on each side.

7.8 miles: More original railroad ties still in their initial place.

8.0 miles: Another rock cut, but this one shows signs of human littering, the first that we've seen on our journey.

8.2 miles: Route 63. Be careful, as this is a busy and dangerous highway. The trail will end at Hop Brook Recreation Site across this road.

6 Stratton Brook Park Trail

Endpoints: Junction of Routes 167 / 309, Simsbury, Connecticut, through Stratton Brook Park, to West Mountain Road, Simsbury Connecticut
Location: Hartford County, town of Simsbury, Connecticut.
Length: 3.0 miles
Surface: Crushed stone and asphalt.

Uses:

To get there: Start at Stratton Brook Park located off Route 309 in Simsbury, Connecticut. Upon entering the Park, follow the road to the end and park near the covered bridge. The trail passes in front of this landmark, which is a convenient starting point, though in the middle of the trail. It is one mile from here to the **east** end of the trail (going left), and two miles to the **west** end of the trail (heading to your right).

Contact:
Dan Dickinson, Supervisor, Stratton Brook State Park
194 Stratton Brook Road
Simsbury, Connecticut 06070
203-242-1158

Gerard Toner, Director
Department of Culture, Parks and Recreation
933 Hopmeadow Street
Simsbury, CT 06070
203-651-3751

Local resources for bike repairs/rentals:
Bicycle Cellar, 532 Hopmeadow Street, Simsbury, 203-658-1311.
Farmington Bicycle Shop, Post Office Sq., Farmington, 203-677-2453.
Neckers, 1591 Hopmeadow Street, Simsbury, 203-658-5783.

The Central New England Railway (CNE) is not a name readily remembered in the late 20th century, so there are few that know it played a major role in the tumultuous and cut-throat times of the late 19th century. The C.N.E. was a line which ran from New York's Hudson River Valley to Hartford, Connecticut, via the rolling hills of Litchfield County, Connecticut.

Quiet pine forest in Simsbury, Connecticut.

The C.N.E. is mainly remembered today for three events: the bridge collapse at Tariffville, Connecticut, the Poughkeepsie High Bridge over the Hudson River, and the trouble on the Tarriffville extension, at Montague farm in East Granby, Connecticut. The Tariffville Disaster happened on the night of January 15, 1878, when a ten-car train of church parishioners was returning home from a night of revival in Hartford. As it was crossing the Farmington River via the twin-span wooden truss bridge, disaster struck: the east span collapsed. One baggage car and three coaches fell into the frozen river. Thirteen people lost their lives that night and seventy were injured. This was the worst train accident in Connecticut's history, and was vividly remembered for many years.

In 1888, after some mergers with other lines in New York, the C.N.E. opened the bridge over the Hudson at Poughkeepsie. This provided a direct route that required no car-floats (ferries) to the coal fields of Pennsylvania. This bridge was the only one south of Albany until the opening of the tunnels and the Hell Gate Bridge in New York City in 1911. The Poughkeepsie High Bridge was in daily use until 1974, when a fire damaged its integrity. It still stands today and is being studied as a possible link in a rail-trail through the beautiful Hudson River Valley.

Small bridge over Stratton Brook near the west end of the trail.

The trouble at Montague Farm, when viewed by sophisticated inhabitants of the late twentieth century, seems almost comic. But from the vantage point of earlier times, it is a tale of high finance, treachery, deceit, and the archetypal rail-baron mentality. At the turn of the century the New Haven Railroad was a powerful corporation that was feared and despised. The underdog C.N.E. was allied with the New York Central, which was then owned by the Vanderbilts. The Tariffville Extension was a fifteen-mile branch to West Springfield in Massachusetts, and a connection with the Boston & Albany (New York Central Railroad). This junction allowed the all-important Pennsylvania coal to be brought far into New England without using the New Haven Railroad, who did not look kindly on this challenge to their traffic base.

As the extension was under construction, a snag developed over a parcel in East Granby, Connecticut. It seems that the owner reneged on the sale to the C.N.E. and instead sold it to Mr. Charles Montague, who then proceeded to tear-up the tracks. He was found to be a front-man for the NH and a court battle ensued. In the meantime, the C.N.E. obtained a right-of-way on an adjoining parcel and completed the branch. Eventually, after a year in court, they won the case and opened the original East Granby routing.

The New Haven was not to be denied, however. As soon as they lost the court case, they proceeded to buy the majority interest in the C.N.E. The NH then had the valuable bridge over the Hudson and they started constructing a line to connect the bridge with their main line into New England. The C.N.E. mainline through the hills of northwestern Connecticut fell into disuse, and it was abandoned in sections starting in the 1930s. Most of the C.N.E. mainline was scrapped in the 1930s and the steel shipped to Japan, where it undoubtedly ended up in the hands of the military. These days, very little of the C.N.E. is still a railroad, and this trail you are about to begin is short, but it will provide some enjoyable features of the old Central New England Railroad that are still visible today.

Covered Bridge at the start of the trail in Stratton Brook Park

6. Stratton Brook State Park

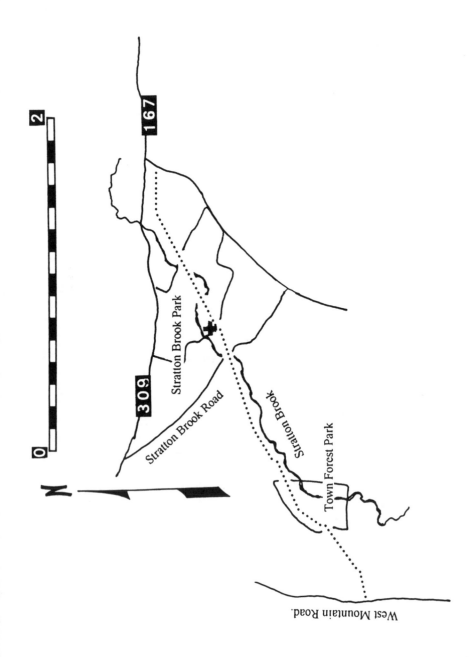

*There are two descriptions that follow, one heading **east**, the other **west**.*

0.0 miles: Using the covered bridge as a starting point and heading **east** (left).

0.1 miles: You are into a young pine forest now and past the ponds.

0.3 miles: Remains of an old rail bridge are seen here. It is the basis for the current bike bridge. As you continue through the forest, Stratton Brook passes underneath as the old railbed is on a little fill, and the brook disappears off to the left.

0.6 miles: Stratton Brook reappears again on the left as you go down-grade.

0.7 miles: Newer housing is in this area with backyards adjoining the trail.

0.9 miles: Access out to Route 309.

1.0 miles: East end of the trail.

(Re-set your odometer)

0.0 miles: Starting at the covered bridge and heading **west** (right). Massacoe Pond is the body of water on your left. Popular with the local fishermen, it provides a tranquil background to the trail. Picnic tables are found here also.

0.1 miles: Stratton Brook turns into a murky slow-moving stream.

0.2 miles: Grade crossing at Stratton Brook Road. The rail-trail is known as Town Forest Road. This is a lightly traveled road so you don't have to worry about a lot of traffic.

0.6 miles: You are now going by a wetland on the right.

0.9 miles: The Town of Simsbury's DPW garage is on the right.

1.0 miles: You are now at the border of Town Forest Park.

1.1 miles: The trail diverges a little to the right and goes across Stratton Brook once again. Look for the remains of the old New Haven bridge abutments under the bridge.

1.2 miles: Grade crossing of Town Forest Road going into woods on the left.

1.3 miles: Going past a baseball field and signs of some coal and cinder from a long ago steam train.

1.4 miles: You're now on a fill and going up-grade.

1.5 miles: A hill rises to the right and a gully is on the left.

1.6 miles: Entering a residential neighborhood and approaching another fill. This one is tall at 25 feet.

1.7 miles: Crossing a small stream via a small culvert. Still going up-grade and approaching another neighborhood.

1.9 miles: Outlet to a *cul de sac* known as Glenbrook Road. Interestingly, this area contains original ballast; small trap rock.

2.0 miles: Trail ends at West Mountain Road.

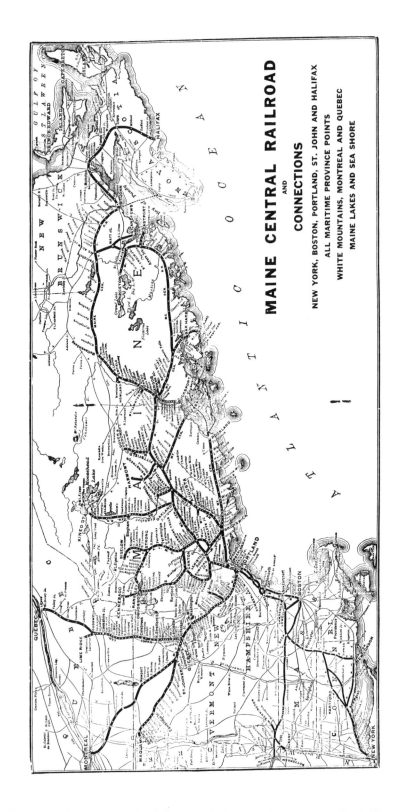

MAINE CENTRAL RAILROAD
AND
CONNECTIONS

NEW YORK, BOSTON, PORTLAND, ST. JOHN AND HALIFAX
ALL MARITIME PROVINCE POINTS
WHITE MOUNTAINS, MONTREAL AND QUEBEC
MAINE LAKES AND SEA SHORE

Great Rail-Trails of Maine

7. Jay-to-Farmington Rail-Trail
8. South Portland Greenbelt

The Jay-to-Farmington Rail-trail is historically important because this was the right-of-way for the Maine Central's branch to Farmington, where a connection was made with the Sandy River and Rangeley Lakes Railroad (SRRL), which was the largest of Maine's famous narrow-gauge railroads. Observable remnants of this line are in Farmington, which today is famous for being the home of the University of Maine. This area is best sampled in the autumn, when the world-famous New England foliage is at peak. It is a special treat to savor the crisp fall air with the scent of pine forest nearby and a wood-burning stove in the distance adding to the pleasure.

The South Portland Trail is a bit different. Here you can examine the urban life on the sea coast of Maine. This trail provides some of the most wide-ranging types of scenery that you'll come across, especially considering it is only a few miles in length. You'll pass by a small rail yard that used to stage tank cars for the trans-loading of petroleum products, and a series of salt water estuaries that support a variety of wildlife that are viewable up-close. You will observe the busy urban center of South Portland, where a clean and shady park is a place to sit and take in the sights. There is even a residential street where residents originally had to look over their shoulders when backing out of driveways to make sure the train wasn't approaching.

Maine's future in the rails-to-trails movement looks promising as there are between 390 and 500 miles of abandoned rail lines. One interesting stretch lies in the Caribou region. Over 70 miles of ex-rail lines are now used by snow mobilers, and the northern Maine economy is enhanced by millions of dollars that these travelers bring to the area. They have recently begun to up-grade these lines for use by summer bikers and horseback riders. A number of other trails are in the planning stages and will be in use in the coming years.

7 Jay-to-Farmington Rail-Trail

Endpoints: Rte 4, Jay, Maine to West Farmington, Maine, with a short road extension to Farmington.
Location: Franklin County Maine. Passing through the towns of Jay, Wilton, and East Wilton, and finishing at either West Farmington or Farmington.
Length: 14.5 miles
Surface: Gravel and cinder

Uses:

To get there: Out of the Portland metropolitan area, take I-95 north, to I-495 north, to exit 12, then follow State Route 4 north to Jay, Maine. Go about one mile past the Jay fire and police stations and you'll see an old rail depot that has been converted into a flower shop. The trail starts here and heads to the right (north). Park where you have permission or it is otherwise approved.

Contact:
Scott D. Ramsey, Supervisor
Off Road Vehicles, Bureau of Parks
Department of Conservation, #22, Augusta, ME 04333
207-287-3821

Local resources for bike repairs/rentals:
Northern Lights, Rte 2 & 4, West Farmington, 207-778-6566.

This trail is not well known outside of Maine, which is a shame because it is an unspoiled and picturesque trail that offers surprises for those who try it. It has some interesting history in addition to the natural beauty of the surroundings.

Last known as the Farmington branch of the Maine Central Railroad (MEC), the line went up here for one primary reason; to connect with the Sandy River and Rangeley Lakes Railroad (SR&RL). This was a 2-foot, narrow-gauge line that started at Farmington, Maine, and went in a generally northern direction on two primary branches. The reason someone would build a railroad that didn't match in size to the gauge of conventional railroads is economics. The narrow-gauge types were cheaper to build and maintain than standard gauge lines, and they were generally built in places that were remote or had mountainous terrain, places where a good road network was not to be found.

Additionally, they usually were railroads that had a lot of origin traffic. Here in western Maine, that meant abundant traffic in pulpwood logs, lumber, and finished goods made from forest products. The SR&RL had an extensive passenger business also, which connected the outside world with Farmington. This Lilliputian railroad was among the country's largest in terms of miles laid (slightly more than 110). During the early years of the century, Farmington was the site of one of the busiest transfer yards in the Northeast. Teams of men, scores of them per shift, would transfer the commodity of every car that came down the SR&RL to the MEC. This was done the old fashioned way, by hand -- not a very efficient transportation system by today's standards, but it worked back then. Of course, by the time the Depression came, the narrow gauge was on thin ice economically and the line was sold and scrapped in 1936.

When the SR&RL folded, the MEC branch lost most of its reason for being there, but continued to hold on until 1982, when it was finally abandoned and pulled up. Guilford Transportation, through their subsidiary, MEC, still owns the land at present, but the State of Maine is in negotiation (at the time of this writing) to purchase the land. The state has managed the site since 1982 and has transformed it into a fine multi-use path. Two local clubs, The Western Maine ATV Association and The Woodland Wanderers have spent literally hundreds of hours doing the necessary regular maintenance on this beautiful site to keep it looking great. The collection of railway equipment from the early era, once stored at Edaville, Massachusetts, is now back at home in Maine. It is now part of the Maine Narrow-gauge Railroad Co. & Museum at Portland, which will be up and running in 1995.

Bridge over Cemetery Street in East Wilton, Maine

7. Jay-to-Farmington Rail-Trail

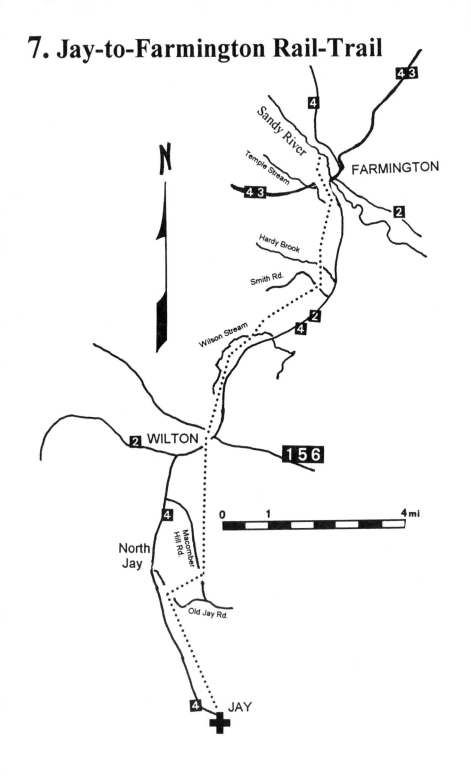

0.0 miles: As you start the trail, a small pond is on the right.

0.1 miles: Grade crossing for a driveway The trail is basically cinder-covered in this section as you go by a residential neighborhood.

0.4 miles: You start to divert some from Rte 4 and head into the woods of Maine. A small wooden timber bridge is here also with concrete abutments. This is only a few feet wide and you'll see plenty of this style of bridge on this trail. A small access trail leads to Rte 4. There are also signs pointing out services and amenities that you'll find on that particular outlet to the "outside world." Don't forget, these trails are used extensively by snowmobilers who travel many miles and have a definite need for these services along the way.

0.7 miles: Power lines cross the trail here. Right back into the woods after the clearing for the lines.

1.0 miles: As you go up-grade on a fill, there is a meadow here with an unusual assortment of wild berries. Peaceful place to stop and enjoy the extraordinary rock formation.

1.5 miles: Beaver activity abounds here. Drowned wetlands and a large hut.

1.7 miles: The trail is wider and firmer in this area. Occasional ties are found now, really the first sign that this was at one time a railroad.

2.0 miles: Grade crossing of Fuller Road. This is a paved highway and has a good amount of cars, so be cautious.

2.2 miles: Rte 4 can be heard, if not seen, off to the left.

2.3 miles: Another one of those small wooden bridges, once again only 6 feet long.

2.4 miles: Jay's Solid Waste Transfer Station is next to you on nearby Rte 4.

2.8 miles: Grade crossing for a place called Bull's Eye Driving Range. The trail in this section is nice and hard with cinder under foot and a wide path to navigate.

3.2 miles: You're still running parallel and adjacent to Rte 4, but now there is a beautiful vista that has opened up beyond the highway. Some of the mountains visible here are Saddleback, Law, and Bald Mountains. An old ramshackle barn on the right side of the trail complements the scene.

3.4-3.5 miles: This is the site of the old North Jay yard. Multiple tracks were here to switch cars for local industries such as milk producers and grain dealers. A cut stone retaining wall is here to hold back a slight rise to the right and the skeletal remains of a building are just beyond. This area is an alternative parking site.

3.7-3.8 miles: A residential neighborhood is here with a grade crossing of Old Jay Road. Just as you cross, a split in the street has an upper route leading to more houses and the lower road leads to Rte 4. More scenic memories are here. The North Jay Water District building is the only municipal or industrial site visible here.

3.9 miles: Another small culvert of the type that is common to this railroad.

4.2 miles: Going up a slight hill now as the highway starts to drop below you and the trail curves to the right.

4.5 miles: Grade crossing of a dirt road known as Macomber Hill Road.

4.6 miles: The largest fill yet is found here. At 35 feet it presents a different perspective to the surroundings.

4.8 miles: A rocky cut is the next feature. Unusual mosses and shade plants.

4.9-5.1 miles: Back onto another fill. This time about 45-50 feet high.

5.2 miles: Grade crossing of a paved country road.

5.3 miles: A small cut with gentle sloping sides.

5.4 miles: Grade crossing for another small country road.

5.9 miles: On a cinder fill here.

6.3 miles: A genuine beaver dam is right next to the trail. Someone has put a gate or screen on the dam to prevent its owners and builders from totally blocking the flow of water.

6.7 miles: The woods are still to the left, but a meadow is on the right.

7.0 miles: Agricultural grade crossing is found here that connects to the big meadow on the right.

7.2 miles: A grade crossing is here with a few houses. A marsh provides a home for the mosquitoes. Another one of those ubiquitous 6-foot bridges.

7.4 miles: Grade crossing of a busy Rte 4 &2 and nearby Rte 156 as you enter the town of Wilton, Maine. Use caution in traffic. Steve's Market is a nice place to get a drink.

ATVs on a Jay Trail bridge.

7.7 miles: Grade crossing of an industrial complex's driveway. Forster Manufacturing has a warehouse that at one time was used to transfer freight between rail and truck.

7.9 miles: On a bit of a fill in this area as Rte 4 & 2 is off to the right and you approach the biggest bridge yet. A nicely constructed, pressure-treated deck is the surface. The bridge itself is of the deck-girder type.

8.1 miles: On a small cinder fill here as you ascend a slight grade.

8.3 miles: Rte 4 is running just next to the trail on the right. Cheapo Depot (yes, that's the name) Furniture Sales is a nearby structure.

8.6 miles: A river winds into view. This is known as Wilson Stream.

9.1 miles: A sign for snowmobiles showing fuel and other services for them.

9.8 miles: Here is an interesting bridge. Very long and narrow, one-way traffic only, particularly if there are ATVs on the trail. This bridge passes over Cemetery Street in East Wilton, and the Wilson Stream. The Hometown Market at the end of the bridge seems to be the old East Wilton Depot, a small structure of definite railroad architecture. It makes for a convenient place to stop and get a drink or otherwise explore this charming town. The falls in the river, just below the bridge, makes for a scenic picture. This and many other photo opportunities are just waiting for a camera. To continue on, go across the street and follow the path of the tracks to the right.

10.0 miles: Grade crossing at a small residential street, known as High Street.

10.2 miles: Forster Company is here as you pass over Mill Street. Believe it or not, this place makes clothes pins for distribution all over the country.

10.4 miles: Agricultural grade crossing is here as you enter an area of a fill with a swampy area on both sides.

10.7 miles: A 25-foot high fill is here, followed by a series of cuts and fills, for about 3/10s mile.

11.0 miles: Grade crossing of Smith Road, followed by another one of those small 6-foot bridges. Cattail grasses in this area.

11.2 miles: On a fill, this one 25' high. Shortly after, back to level ground.

11.8 miles: On a cinder fill here (25-50 ft.) with undulating ground below.

11.9 miles: The pond here has lily pads where frogs sit and view the passersby.

12.0 miles: A grade crossing of a steep road is here. A valley is to the right with Rte 4 in the distance.

12.1 miles: Crossing a 40-foot deck-girder bridge that spans a mountain stream known as Hardy Brook, which is rushing down to the valley.

12.3 miles: On a cinder fill again that isn't very high.

12.8 miles: Passing a marsh on the right.

13.3 miles: Trail bends to the right as it avoids the marsh on the left.

13.7 miles: Beaver activity is evident with the high water here.

14.0 miles: Bridge over the Temple Stream. Over 100 feet in length and 70 feet above the water, this is an impressive deck-girder span. As you cross into West Farmington, you'll come upon C.N. Brown, a fuel oil dealer that one time received deliveries by rail.

Waterfall and houses in East Wilton, Maine.

14.3 miles: The power equipment dealer's building was at one time a freight house. Across the street is an old, forlorn, passenger station, which seems to have been moved to its present site, but not restored yet. Maxwell's Citgo Station is just up the street from the old passenger station and available for food, drink, and conversation. Continue on the trail by crossing over the highway only if you are on foot or bicycle. No motorized vehicles are allowed on this final short stretch.

14.5 miles: Here you are at the Sandy River and overlooking the piers of the bridge that once was here. The bridge was damaged in the floods of the spring of 1987 and it was closed to trail traffic at that time. It was finally torn down in 1990. You can see into Farmington proper and the route of the MEC interchange point. This area stands about 60 feet over the river and it makes for a fine place to sit and contemplate life. If you so desire, you can continue on to Farmington from here.

To get to Farmington: Go back to the grade crossing at Rte 43 and turn left. Follow this down the hill and then take a left across the river. Just after the McDonald's Restaurant, take a left onto Front Street. Here you'll find some restored buildings that were part of the freight trans-loading operations and interchange traffic for the narrow-gauge line. Included here is the old restored passenger station, now serving as a home to a variety of social agencies.

If you look behind the station, you'll see the right-of-way of the MEC track that came in from the Sandy River crossing. The elevated road-bed was at one time a timber causeway, but it was eventually filled by the railroad in the early 1900s. This causeway led to a wye track just before Front Street, where a four-stall engine-house provided service to the Maine Central's power. The Sandy River and Rangeley Lakes Railroad left this area and headed north along the river and crossed over Route 4 on the north side of town. Today, Framington is the home of the University of Maine at Farmington, located one block in from Front Street. Both the University and the downtown area have beautiful views of the mountains of western Maine.

Agricultural grade
crossing on the Jay trail

8 South Portland Greenbelt

Endpoints: From Elm Street to Stanford Street, within the city limits of South Portland, Maine.
Location: Cumberland County, South Portland, Maine.
Length: 2.0 miles
Surface: Asphalt (small initial length is dirt)

Uses:

To get there: Get off the Maine Turnpike at exit 7and go past Maine Mall Road. Get on Broadway which is just after the I-295 overpass and follow this east towards South Portland center. You will pass over the end of the Boston & Maine Railroad's Rigby Yard and go approximately 1.5 miles beyond. You will then take a left turn onto Elm Street. Go 5 blocks and you come upon a set of tracks between Forest Avenue and Atlantic Avenue. This is the start of the trail. Park where it is safe and approved. The trail heads to the east, to the right.

Contact:
City Manager, City Hall
25 Cottage Road, South Portland, ME 04106
207-767-3201

Local resources for bike repairs/rentals:
Joe Jones Sports, 198 Maine Mall Rd., South Portland, 207-885-5635.
Yankee Sports, 35 Foden Road, South Portland, 207-773-0857.

View of the Portland, Maine, sky-line from the rail-trail.

This trail is a piece of beauty within the urban area of South Portland. It may present a bit of a challenge to find, but when you do, it will be worth the trip. This was once an industrial branch of the Portland Terminal Company, a shortline with about 20 miles of track in the Portland, Maine, metropolitan area. This company was set-up jointly by the Maine Central Railroad and the Boston & Maine Railroad, to handle the switching at both the large Rigby Yard in South Portland, owned by the B&M, and industries in Portland served by the Maine Central. When the two large railroads were taken over by Guilford Transportation Industries in the early 1980s, the P.T. Co. was taken over by the Guilford entity, Springfield Terminal Railroad. The oil terminals that provided much of the traffic on this branch found trucks to be more reliable so the line was pulled up in 1984, and the right-of-way converted to become the South Portland Greenbelt.

Pedestrian and 4-legged friend on the South Portland Greenbelt

8. South Portland Greenbelt

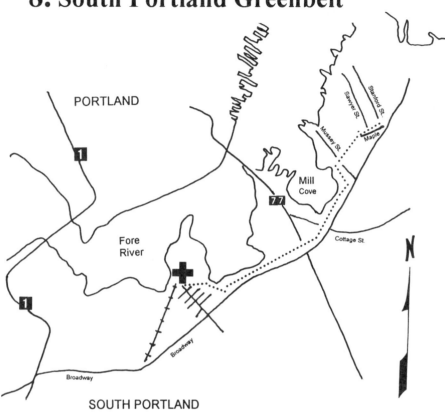

0.0 miles: Grade crossing at Forest Avenue. This initial stage of the trail is a dirt path alongside the railroad tracks. Interesting and abundant wild flowers grow between the rails here. Grade crossing at Chestnut Street is the next major landmark. At the outset of this trail you'll notice that this is an urban area. The residents who abut the trail are sociable and interesting to talk with. Riding this trail will be a memorable experience.

0.1 miles: Oil tank farm is found here and the track is still in place to serve this industry. In the summer of 1994, there was no longer any service to this area. This section is the start of the paved portion of the trail. Also found here is a grade crossing for Pearl Street, and the Fore River comes into view. This river is the border between South Portland and Portland, and it is the reason the tank farm is here. The maritime trade is a major factor in the economy of the Portland area and the route that this trail follows is the route to the sea. The trail provides a sense of the sea and the interwoven trail of commerce that the railroad provided.

0.2 miles: Going past the end of Mildred Street. Both Mildred Street and Pearl Street have outlets for bikes to the trail. The people who live on these small side-streets love the trail, the view, and will tell you all about the comings and goings in South Portland. The tidal inlet that is adjacent to the trail will fill your lungs with the salty scent of the ocean. As you get underway again, the trail starts to go up hill slightly here.

0.3 miles: Going past the end of Morse Street now, with an access to the trail found here. Shortly after is the grade crossing at Bagley Street. Summer wildflowers and berry bushes abound here. The waterfront is still very visible.

0.4 miles: The trail is winding downhill in this area.

0.5 miles: The trail is very close to Broadway as you pass by a Saab service garage. The trail passes over a tidal pool by way of a bent-timber type bridge. These are not seen very often on rail-trails because they are an old design, and for the most part, they disappeared from the scene long before the rail-trail movement came into being.

0.6 miles: The trail starts to diverge from the highway and then the trail arrives at downtown South Portland. This is an extremely busy area, so be careful as you cross the major intersection at Waterman Drive.

0.9 miles: South Portland Rose Garden is adjacent to you now. This is a beautiful park and a good place to "stop and smell the roses." This park is clean, well-kept, and has a lavish selection of roses, perennials, and annuals.

1.0 miles: A small bridge is traversed and a pond is visible in the Park. Nearby is a residential house that has a gorgeous formal garden abutting the trail.

1.1 miles: Grade crossing at Cottage Street. A small tidal canal is adjacent to you; the picturesque Portland skyline is visible also. A plaque commemorating the construction of the rail-trail is here.

1.3 miles: The trail winds to the left and comes close to the waterfront at Mill Cove. A residential neighborhood is on the right with commanding views of this striking scene. An interesting bit of construction is seen here: the retaining wall was fabricated by the railroad out of diamond plate steel sheets and old rails. This is seen in other places along the way.

1.5 miles: Trail is still winding around the cove and going uphill. An old industrial complex is on the left, part of which is now a United States Coast Guard facility.

1.6 miles: Grade crossing at Mussey Street thru a residential neighborhood.

1.7 miles: Grade crossing at Harriet Street and shortly after is Roosevelt Street. A nice field with plenty of beautiful wildflowers and ball field is on your right.

1.8 miles: The trail heads onto Maple Street. The rail and ties are still under the pavement which makes for a bumpy block.

1.9 miles: Grade crossing at Sawyer Street.

2.0 miles: Grade crossing at Stanford Street. This is effectively the end of the true rail-trail as the remainder of the right-of-way is blocked by a fence and rails are still in place on this isolated segment. Perhaps this section is slated to be completed in the coming years.

Woodside Avenue Bridge, Norwottuck trail, Amherst, Massachusetts

Great Rail-Trails of Massachusetts

9. Ayer to Dunstable
10. Barre to Templeton
11. Cape Cod Rail-Trail
12. Minuteman Rail-Trail
13. Northampton Bikeway
14. Norwottuck Rail-Trail
15. Shining Sea Rail-Trail

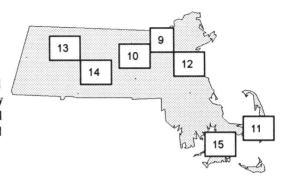

The rail-trails of Massachusetts seem to be the most extensively developed and completed of all the trails in New England. An active government agency in the Department of Environmental Management, Division of Resource Conservation, has a Bikeway and Trail Planning section run by Dan O'Brien. He is always in the forefront at community meetings, helping to make his office more responsive to the needs and concerns of the various communities that benefit from the rail-trails in Massachusetts.

Massachusetts has one of the oldest rail-trails, Cape Cod (1979), as well as one of the newest, Norwottuck (1993). As you travel these, you will notice the developed network of ancillary services available to the trail user that have sprung up along the older Cape Cod Trail, as compared with fewer services that are exclusively directed to trail users of the newer Norwottuck Trail. It will be interesting to see if enterprising business people take advantage of capturing the Norwottuck Trail market.

The scenery along Massachusetts rail-trails is varied. It runs the gamut, from the perfectly-manicured, ocean-front Shining Sea Trail, to the rustic and forested Barre to Templeton Trail, where you'll rarely see houses or people. The urban-to-suburban scope of the Minuteman Trail is complemented by the historical value of Lexington and its proximity to Boston. Massachusetts rail-trails are also a fun way to see some of the small, out-of-the-way communities like Florence on the City of Northampton Bikeway, or Groton and Pepperell on the Ayer-to-Dunstable Trail.

The Great Rail-Trails of Massachusetts are gems waiting for you to discover.

9 Ayer To Dunstable Rail-Trail

Endpoints: Main and Park Streets, Ayer, Massachusetts. Ending at the border with Hollis, New Hampshire, between Groton Road and the Nashua River.
Location: Middlesex County, Ayer, Groton, Pepperell, and Dunstable
Length: 10.8 miles
Surface: Gravel

Uses:

To get there: Follow Route 2 to the exit for Route 110 and 111 to Ayer. After about 2 miles you'll come to a rotary. Follow signs for Ayer, which is about another 2 miles ahead. At Main Street and Park Street, there is a Fleet Bank, and the trail starts out back. Park only in approved or safe areas.
Contact:
George Kahale
Montachusett Regional Planning Commission
Room 1427, Water Street
Fitchburg, MA 01420
508-345-7376 or 345-2216
Local resources for bike repairs/rentals:
Mike's Bikes
38 Main Street, Pepperell, MA
508-433-3033

This trail is somewhat different than the majority of the "official" Rail-trails, in that it is not a finished, improved product. On this trail you may encounter some deep water that you will be able to avoid but it can be challenging. In the hey-day of the railroads, Ayer, Massachusetts, was a hot-bed of activity. Branch lines of the B&M radiated out of town, like so many spokes of a wagon-wheel. The following is a list of these lines, and the spoke of their activity is the subject of this chapter.

(1) The Freight Main Line, the main east-west line of the B & M, runs through the center of Ayer.
(2) The Lowell Junction Branch; starting at the "Willows," just east of Ayer, runs to Lowell and serves some vital industry to this day.
(3) The Greenville Branch runs only as far as West Groton. Most of this branch is known today as the Mason Rail-Trail.
(4) The Worcester Branch, an active line, connects the Freight Main with Conrail's Boston & Albany Division via Barber's Junction just outside Worcester.
(5) The Hollis Branch ran across the main street of the Ayer and due north, passing through Groton, Pepperell, and Dunstable on the way to the small town of Hollis, New Hampshire.

The Hollis Branch was originally part of the Worcester & Nashua Railroad. Built in 1848 to connect Worcester with the Fitchburg Railroad (predecessor of the B&M) and onward to the industry of the Merrimack Valley. In the early days it ran to Portland through Nashua, but it was reorganized a number of times. Finally in 1886 it was absorbed into the B&M. Around the turn of the century, the line supported over a dozen passenger trains a day between Worcester and Nashua. By the early 1930s, passenger traffic dwindled, and just one trip each way was on the schedule. 1934 saw the last passenger train-run north of Ayer, and the section between Nashua and Hollis was out of service by 1936 and formally abandoned in 1942.

Hollis had the archetypal New England depot that served the local farmers and small shippers of "less-than-carload" freight. This business, as small as it was, allowed the line to stay open for many years. However, the majority of the freight business was in the Pepperell area, with a couple of small paper mills as the mainstay. But this dwindled also, and the line was abandoned all the way back to Ayer in 1982. The state of Massachusetts acquired the right-of-way in 1987 and has planned to up-grade the drainage on the trail in 1995.

Grade Crossing near the New Hampshire border

9. Ayer to Dunstable

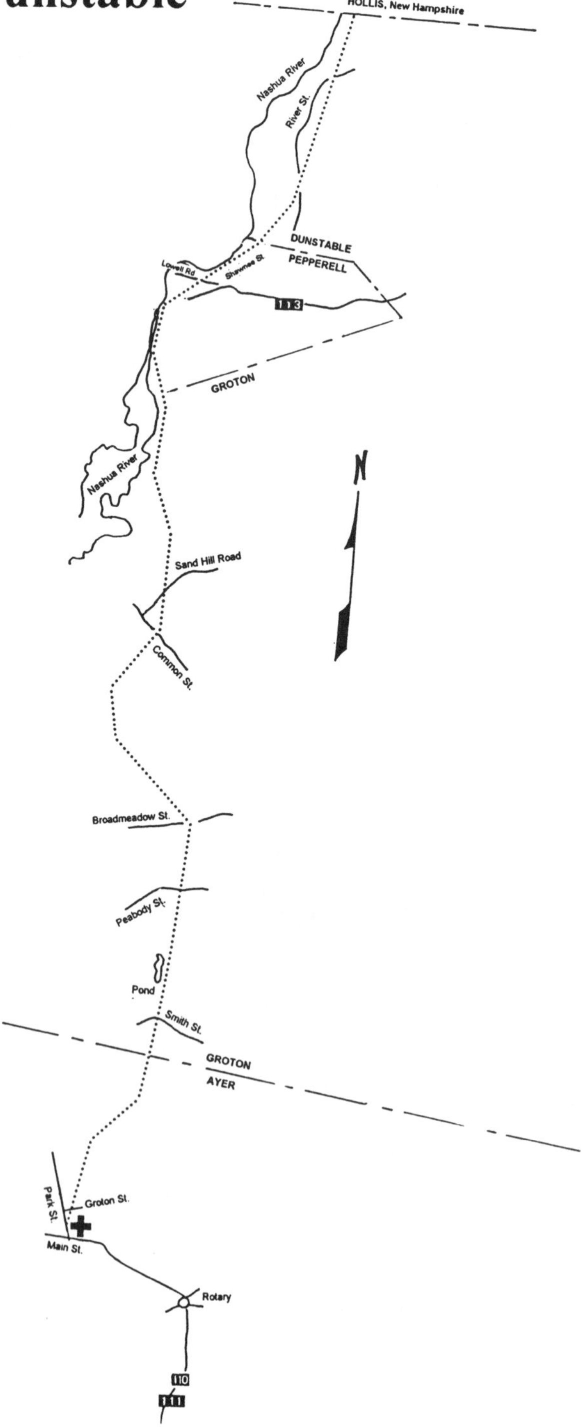

HOLLIS, New Hampshire

Nashua River

River St.

DUNSTABLE

PEPPERELL

Lowell Rd.   Shawnee St.

113

GROTON

Nashua River

N

Sand Hill Road

Common St.

Broadmeadow St.

Peabody St.

Pond

Smith St.

GROTON

AYER

Park St.   Groton St.

Main St.

Rotary

110

111

0.0 miles: In Ayer you'll find that the trail is grass-covered and a well-worn path. Some industries used to be in this area in days past and can still be discerned from the parallel running Route 111.

0.1 miles: Grade crossing at Groton Street. Horne Packaging Corporation is here. This looks to have been a rail-served industry at one time. You will also find a barrier across the trail here to keep out the autos. It will be a little sandy in the next section, so be prepared.

0.5 miles: Power lines traverse the trail in this area, along with the first of some peaceful forests. Large puddles may be in this section also, depending on how much rain has fallen recently.

0.7miles: Out of the forest and into an open area.

0.9 miles: Into more puddles again near a granite B & M type whistle marker.

1.0 miles: Residential neighborhood is on the left and Jonathan Drive is the nearest street. The right side of the trail, past the tree line, is an open meadow.

1.1 mile: Small pond on the right and you are on a fill about 15 feet high and unusually wide; the railroad was double-tracked in this area.

1.2 miles: Crossing under some power lines again.

1.4 miles: On a fill here and going slightly uphill.

1.7 miles: Still uphill and on the fill. A vernal pool is on the right and just beyond the trees is another delightful meadow.

1.8 miles The fill is higher, now approaching 30 feet high.

2.0 miles: Grade crossing of Smith Street. The boundary with Groton was just before this. The fill and the up-grade are gone now.

2.2 miles: A refreshing pond is on the left. Great Blue Herons can be seen here in the summer months. Smaller pond on the right and more of the rolling meadows you've witnessed previously. The Nashoba Valley region is known for its apples and you are coming upon one of its orchards.

2.5 miles: Trail narrows up and you are entering a bit of a cut.

2.6 miles: Coming up on a large puddle. Depending upon the time of year, this may be deep. A horse path is to the left; going off the trail will lead you around this obstacle.

2.8 miles: Still off the rail-trail and on the horse trail. A small bridge will appear here and a fork. Go to the right and this will lead towards the rail-trail.

3.1 miles: You are now out of the woods and onto Peabody Street. Here you will find the first of two "tunnels" on this trail. Culverts may be a better term and it may be very wet when you come upon this area.

3.3 miles: Past the bad section that can be flooded but not impassable. Fairly open in this area; the trail is wide also, perhaps another passing siding was here. Off to the right and visible through the trees is Route 225/119 as you approach Groton center.

3.6 miles: Small culvert here allows water to flow from one side of the trail to the other.

3.7 miles: Grade crossing of Broadmeadow Street. Impressive willow trees. Groton's passenger and freight station and a small yard were here at one time. Today this site is the headquarters of the Groton Electric Light Department. A small building off to the side that has a rail-flavored architecture serves as the Lineman Training Facility for New England Public Power Associates. Also in this area is the Buckingham Bus Lines, which uses an old rail freight building for their garage.

4.1 miles: Here you'll find an old coal dealer with the remains of the trestle used to transfer the coal. Now known as May and Haley fuel oil dealer.

4.2 miles: You're back into the woods again.

4.3 miles: Crossing under Route 111 through the second of the tunnel / culverts.

4.4 miles: An attractive colonial type farmhouse with interesting features.

4.7 miles: If you pass by this trail in the summer, you'll be pleasantly surprised by the lovely wildflowers which abound in this section.

4.9 miles: Here are the abutments for an overpass that has been torn down, possibly the West Street bridge.

5.1 miles: You are now on a fill which approaches the bridge over Rte 111-119. This is a thru-girder bridge with the large ballast still in place.

5.3 miles: The trail is narrowing up, with the surface starting to deteriorate into the dreaded wash-board effect for a short while.

5.5 miles: Agricultural grade crossing which leads to the beautiful horse farms and meadows on both sides.

5.7 miles: Grade crossing at Common Street, then a big fill, about 25 ft. high.

5.9 miles: Horse farm on the left.

6.2 miles: Grade crossing at Sand Hill Road.

6.4 miles: On a fill again as the trail widens up in a mature forest. There is also an old concrete B & M rail rack in this area. These were used to store rails in an area that was prone to problems.

6.5 miles: Here is an old B&M mile marker with the inscription "34," which means 34 miles to Boston.

7.3 miles: This area is the Rich State Park.

7.7 miles: The water on the left is the Nashua River. This secluded oasis is the drawing card for the State Forest. You can walk down to the shore and take in the tranquil beauty.

7.9 miles: Here is an interesting feature. The builders of this railroad decided to cut through the hill on the right and totally remove the hill's remains on the left.

8.1 miles: Still going past the Nashua River.

8.7 miles: You are in downtown Pepperell now, with the line of shops straight ahead. This road is Route 113. Notice the dam which impounds the Nashua River. It's a typical New England mill-town scene. The trail continues past the downtown area.

8.8 miles: Here is Railroad Street on your left and parallel to you. In a short distance you will cross Lowell Road.

8.9 miles: As the Nashua River meanders closer, and Shawnee Street is parallel on the left, you are in the area of a junction with a branch that crossed over the river to a mill.

9.1 miles: This is the town border of Dunstable.

9.6 miles: Grade crossing at River Street.

10.3 miles: Grade crossing again of River Street.

10.8 miles: Border with Hollis, New Hampshire, and the end of the trail.

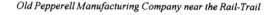

Old Pepperell Manufacturing Company near the Rail-Trail

10 Barre To Templeton Rail-Trail

Endpoints: Route 122, at the Barre / Oakland, Massachusetts town line and ending at Route 2A Templeton, Massachusetts.
Location: Worcester County, Massachusetts, towns of Barre, Hubbardston, Phillipston, Templeton.
Length: 12.1 miles
Surface Gravel and original ballast. Some ties still in place.

Uses:

To get there: East of Quabbin Reservoir, pick-up MA 122. Just north of Barre proper, and right at the Oakham town line, you'll notice a series of piers that used to support a bridge across the Ware River. On the left side of the highway you can park at the fishing area that is adjacent to the rail-trail which heads northeast, away from the river.
Contact:
Dan O'Brien, Bikeway and Trail Planner, Dept. of Environmental Management
Division of Resource Conservation
100 Cambridge Street Room 104
Boston, MA 02202
617-727-3160 ext 557

Local resources for bike repairs/rentals:
Country Bike,12 Exchange Street, Barre, MA 508-355-2219

During the mid-19th century, the state of Massachusetts had two major east-west railroad lines. The Western Railroad's Boston & Albany line opened in 1867 and today is known as Conrail. The Fitchburg System, which opened in 1875, is known today as "The Freight Main" of the Boston & Maine Railroad. These competing roads ran parallel through Massachusetts about thirty miles apart, with the B&A in the south and the B&M on the northern tier. It was logical that feeder lines were built to interconnect them.

One of these subsidiary lines started in the western Massachusetts town of Palmer, connected with the B&A, was known as the Ware River Railroad and ran as far as the town of Gilbertville, about 15 miles. This was eventually taken over by the B&A, and construction was begun to take the line to Baldwinville near Winchendon, where a connection was made with the B&M.

A significant amount of traffic crossed this area. The towns of Ware and Barre had large mill complexes that benefited immensely by being located so close to two large railroads. But by the middle of the 20th century, a decline in the textile and paper industry was in full swing in New England and the death knell was sounding for the mills of the Ware River Valley. When Penn-Central was formed in 1968, it set out to abandon any and all branches that were not carrying their weight. The Ware River Secondary, as this line was called, was among the first to be cast off. The rails were pulled up around this time and today the State of Massachusetts owns the land.

This is not an official rail-trail; it is not a finished and manicured path. Instead, what you'll find here is a nicely forested, quiet place to walk or have a fun mountain-bike ride. This trail is not really do-able all the way to the junction with the B&M because Route 2 is a fairly new highway constructed across the right-of-way with no provision made for a safe crossing. It is worth mentioning that this trail is in the Ware River Watershed area, which drains into the Quabbin Reservoir, the main source of water for metropolitan Boston.

0.3 miles: You start out in a pine forest and are going over a culvert. Remnants of ties are scattered about, giving the surroundings a railroad "feel." The trail in this area is pleasantly wide and smooth.
0.6 miles: An old wire fence follows you as you come upon a small fill.
0.8 miles: A small cut is encountered here along with an up-grade.
1.1 miles: In this area you are on a shelf with the river on the right.
1.5 miles: Here you come upon a quarry that is active but not too large.
1.7 miles: Look past the tree-line on the right, you'll see Riverside Cemetery. This section also has a grade crossing that is a driveway to a nearby house.
2.2 miles: Small dirt road crosses over the trail.
2.5 miles: Grade crossing at a hard-packed, well traveled dirt road. The ties are in the ground in this section which makes for a challenging bike ride. You may prefer to use the path on the side.

The piers on Ware River once supported the rail bridge at the Oakham-Barre border.

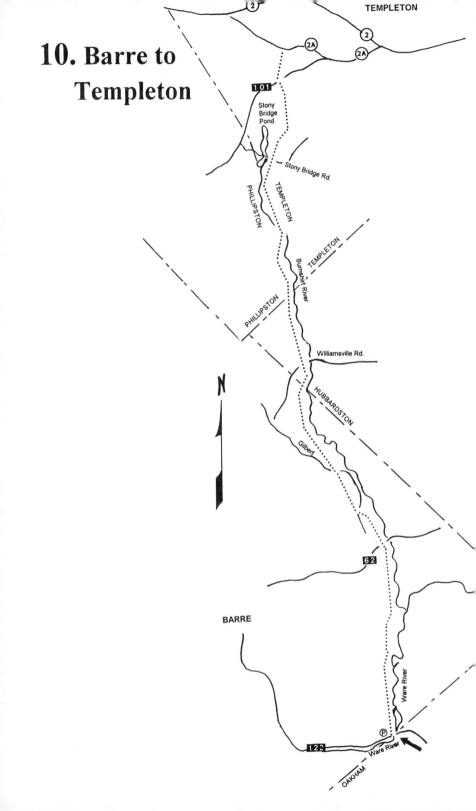

10. Barre to Templeton

2.7 miles: Small fill with a culvert. Be on the look-out for the small signs and markers. This is part of the a snowmobile path.

3.2 miles: Grade crossing at Granger Road. This is a dirt road which meets at an oblique angle.

3.3 miles: Grade crossing at Route 62, a busy paved road.

3.4 miles: On a fill now as you approach a grade crossing at Gilbert Road, another dirt road. It gets a little bumpy here with the washboard effect.

3.8 miles: Grade crossing at Gilbert Road again as we wind up the river valley.

4.3 miles: On a fill again with a pine forest and more ties off to the side.

4.5 miles: Stone wall foundation for a long-abandoned house is visible on the left. The trail is cinder in this area which makes for a better ride.

4.7 miles: Gentle stream crosses under you now via a culvert.

5.1 miles: Concrete culvert is here and the ties are still in place.

5.6 miles: Up-grade and the trail smooths out as you parallel the river valley.

5.9 miles: This is the border with Hubbardston, as you come into a residential neighborhood with a grade crossing at Williamsville Road. A gate here prevents cars from entering the rail-trail.

6.0 miles: The trail might be a little wet in this area because of poor drainage.

6.1 miles: This area is wide open and grass-covered.

6.2 miles: Here is a fill as the trail narrows up and the woods encroach again. Williamsville Pond is in this area on the right.

6.3 miles: Cinder and coal are on the trail and hardwood trees are in majority.

6.5 miles: The river is on the right, a lovely scene to observe.

7.2 miles: The forest reverts back to pine and other softwoods as the river is below and to the right. Here also you enter into Phillipston.

7.7 miles: The river drops down as the trail rises up and bends to the left.

7.9 miles: A gravel quarry here with some intersecting roads to access it.

8.5 miles: A little fill is here with some logging roads also. Ties are in place.

8.7 miles: On a fill again as we approach a bridge over the Burnshirt River. This bridge is a deck-girder type with the original wooden decking still in place. This section also marks the border with Templeton.

9.1 miles: The wash board effect is in this area.

9.4 miles: Another quarry is here along with a stone culvert under the trail.

10.0 miles: Grade crossing at Stoney Bridge Road.

10.4 miles: Ties are found in place and a small path is on the side.

10.9 miles: Grade crossing at a dirt road which leads to another quarry. The ties seem to disappear here and the trail smooths out.

11.3 miles: Meadow on the right as you come upon a small fill.

11.5 miles: Grade crossing at Route 101, Petersham Road. This is a busy road and there is a residential neighborhood located here also. The ties are still in place on the other side of the highway.

12.0 miles: You come upon a rail-served cement plant that made pre-formed stairs. It is an eerie sentinel of past employment and present vandalism.

12.1 miles: This is Route 2A and the effective end of this trail.

11 Cape Cod Rail-Trail

Endpoints: Dennis, Massachusetts, to Eastham, Massachusetts
Location: Barnstable County. Passing through the towns of Dennis, Orleans, Brewster and Eastham.
Length: 19.2 miles (2 miles on-street in Orleans)
Surface: Asphalt

Uses:

To get there: To start in Dennis: Take Route 6 to Exit 9 onto Route 134 South. Parking area will be a short distance on the left, marked by a sign denoting the Cape Cod Rail-Trail.
To start in Brewster: Take Route 6 to Exit 12 onto Route 6A West. Follow signs to Nickerson State Park and upon entry park at first area on the right.

Contact:
Steve Nicolle, Park Manager
Nickerson State Park
Main Street
Brewster, Massachusetts 02361
508-896-3491
Local resources for bike repairs/rentals:
Brewster; Palmer Cycle, 454 Main Street, 508-385-9044
Brewster; Rail-trail Bike Shop, 302 Underpass Road, 508-896-8200
Eastham; Little Capistrano Bike Shop, Salt Pond Road, 508-255-6515
Orleans; Cape Cod Divers, Rte-6A, 508-432-9035
Orleans; Orleans Cycle, 26 Main Street, 508-255-9115

Cape Cod conjures up visions of quaint New England villages, cranberry bogs, small ponds, sand dunes, and meadows of tall grasses intermingled with wild flowers. This place is a hiker's or bicyclist's paradise, but the best way to take it all in is on the Cape Cod Rail-Trail.

The trail follows the path of the Old Colony Railroad that was completed as far as Wellfleet by 1870. By 1873 it was running to Provincetown, and the boom in tourism to the Cape was in full swing. It was possible at this time to travel to Provincetown from Boston (a distance of 120 miles) in 5 hours, a miraculously short time. In 1893 the New York, New Haven and Hartford Railroad took over and this became its "Old Colony Division."

The automobile bridges over the Cape Cod Canal were opened in 1935, and the end was in sight for the rail passenger business. But the plush trains with such famous names as Cape Codder and Neptune ran until 1959, when increasing competition from the automobile and buses forced the service to be abandoned. In 1960, the line above North Eastham was abandoned even to freight service. In 1965 the section that the bike trail now occupies was formally abandoned by the New Haven. Rail service continues today, however, as a freight railroad in the name of Bay Colony Railroad with customers as far as South Dennis. Scheduled passenger service continues to run as far as Hyannis via Amtrak. The Cape Cod Scenic Railroad operates a tourist train between the Cape Cod Canal and Hyannis. Both are only operational in the summer months.

Since 1979 the Cape Cod Rail-Trail has been managed by the State Department of Environmental Management and is a role model for others trails across the country. This is a unique trail in that there are many points along the way to start, and various things to do along the way. We will start in Dennis.

Parking lot at Dennis shows the popularity of the trail

11. Cape Cod Rail-Trail

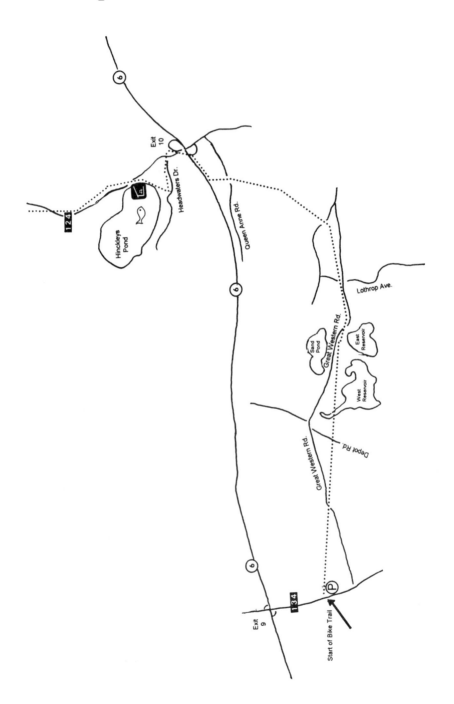

0.1 miles: We are in a beautiful forest with many fragrant pines and a serene quiet that is refreshing to experience after the journey to get here.

0.2 miles: The ubiquitous stone marker is here warning the engineer to signal his presence at the approaching Dennis passenger station, which used to be where the parking lot is now.

0.6 miles: Grade crossing of Great Western Road. Use caution: a busy road.

1.3 miles: Depot Street is crossed here as you pass into Harwich. In this area also is an old mill complex that was rail-served. Now known as Mid Cape Grain, it seems to be a distributor of pet foods.

1.5 miles: Here can be found the ruins of a coaling trestle.

1.8 miles: You are passing by the West Reservoir. In the spring months of April and May, alewives return here to spawn, coming from the ocean to the south via Herring River.

2.0 miles: Grade crossing of Bells Neck Road, a dirt road.

2.2 miles: On a fill in this area that is notable for its height of about 15 feet. Sand Pond is on the left and East Reservoir is in the woods off to the right.

2.3 miles: Grade crossing of Great Western Road again as you continue east.

2.5 miles: Agricultural grade crossing to get into a cranberry field. If you're here in mid-September you can view the harvest, which involves flooding the field with water from nearby Sand Pond. The cranberries then float to the top and allow for mechanical harvesting. Also note the numerous bird houses which provide a haven for song birds in the summer.

2.8 miles: Grade crossing of Lothrup Avenue, next to Great Western Road.

3.1 miles: Here you are on a bit of a fill which crosses a low-lying area and start to diverge from the accompanying road.

3.2 miles: On your left you will note the old rail-served lumber facility with its old style storage sheds and work areas. Some work is still done here, but doesn't seem to be retail, only a job shop. Shortly after this complex is a culvert under Main Street. You will see the New Haven abutments that have partially been filled over as the bridge was taken out and replaced with a fill within the last few years. On the other side of the road you will note a wider area and a path diverging away to the right. This area was once the junction for the Chatham branch. Abandoned in 1937, this 8-mile spur once took passengers to the eastern most tip of the Cape. In its hey-day it carried 23,000 customers every summer. Planning is underway to extend the trail in that direction. The construction is scheduled to begin in 1995.

4.3 miles: Cross underneath Queen Anne Road, as you are getting closer to the Main Cape Highway. A lot of Scrub Pines are growing in this area, along with abundant mountain laurel.

4.4 miles: Here the trail curves to the right to get around the Highway. You will be on city streets for a while now so be careful of traffic and watch for the signs indicating "Bike Route" and you'll be OK.

Culvert under Main St. and the plantings that highlight the area.

5.0 miles: You're now crossing over the Highway and shortly the rail-trail will reappear on the left at Headwaters Drive. The rail-trail will fork off to the right in a short while.

5.7 miles: Beautiful Hinckleys Pond is on the left. This pond, in addition to being a fine swimming area, provides water to flood the cranberry field on the right. In this area you will also cross over Route 124 and find the Pleasant Lake General Store. With its congenial ambiance and cold sodas you will be tempted to rest and view the pond from its picnic tables.

6.3 miles: Grade crossing of Sequattom Road. The big pond on your right is Long Pond. In the summer, this is a haven for Hobie-Cat sail boats. The pond on the left is Seymour Pond. With its life-guard stations and lovely beach, it makes for an inviting place on a hot summer day.

6.8 miles: Once again a grade crossing of Route 124. Also in the area is the border with Brewster, and you are getting close to Nickerson State Park.

7.1 miles: You cross over Route 124 again and at the same time, Blackberry Lane.

7.4 miles: You are running parallel with Route 124 and going up slight grade.

7.6 miles: Grade crossing at Fisherman's Landing Road.

8.1 miles: On a fill which is tall for this trail at 12 feet.

8.3 miles: Crossing under power-lines which have service roads.

11. Cape Cod Rail-Trail

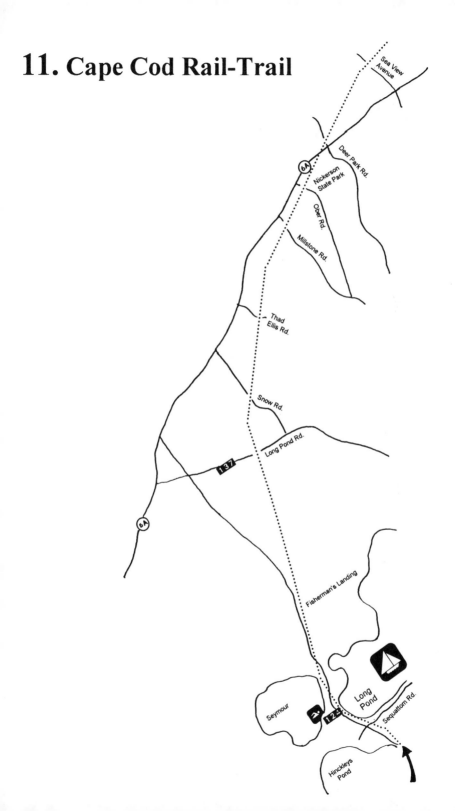

Jog and dog: a natural combo on the rail-trails

9.0 miles: Grade crossing at Long Pond Road, which is also known as Route 137. Here at the corner of Underpass Road and 137, the Brewster Depot stood until it was torn down just prior to World War II. Today in this neighborhood stands the "Candy Store and Country Market," which is a general store and a bike rental shop, in addition to being a U.S. Post Office. This grade crossing also marks the crest of the hill your legs probably have noticed for the past mile and a half.

9.3 miles: Grade crossing of Snow Road. Rail-trail Bike Rentals is in this area along with the famous Brewster Express, a place to get a bite to eat or just relax and people-watch for a while.

10.2 miles: Grade crossing of Thad Ellis Road. An herbarium and organic food store is on this street and may be worth a visit.

10.4 miles: Grade crossing of Old Colony Road.

11 miles: Another grade crossing. This time it's Mill Stone Road.

11.3miles: Now you pass a cut.

11.4 miles: Grade crossing at Ober Road.

11.7 miles: You now are at the Entrance to Nickerson State Park. Here you can find restrooms and information. As you get underway again you will be going under Route 6A by way of a culvert, definitely the safest way to get across.

11.9 miles: Grade crossing again. This time it's Deer Park Road.

12.2 miles: As you're going through a cut in this area, notice the canopy of trees that provide shade here. You are on a fill that is 30 feet high. Stop and note the brook running through the fill and under the trail.

12.6 miles: Grade crossing of Sea View Avenue. Here you can see a small cut with the usual group of scrub pines for cover.

Tranquil pond as viewed from the trail.

11 Cape Cod Rail-Trail

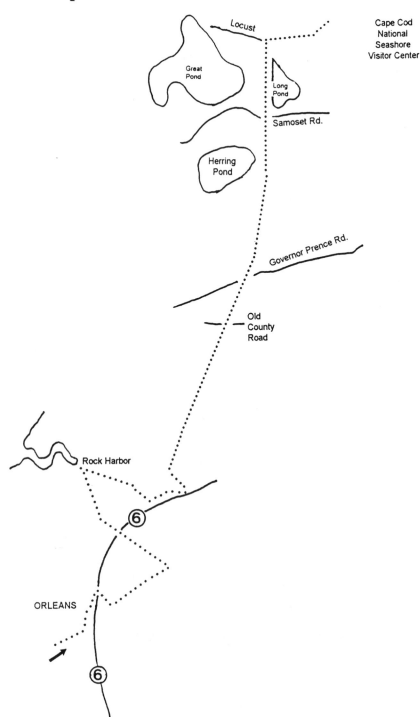

12.9 miles: Small bridge over a marsh and then onto an 8-foot high fill.

13.1 miles: The fill grows higher and the marsh more extensive on each side.

13.3 miles: You are now in Orleans and onto the longest section of the trail that is on public roadways. Be aware of signs denoting the trail and look out for the cars. Planning is underway to get the trail off public roads and onto the town-owned railroad right-of-way.

13.6 miles: You are crossing over Route 6 again and will be taking a left just after the overpass.

14.2 miles: Once again on the rail-bed, you'll be passing Mid Cape Lumber. This was a major customer of the New Haven and they still have a gate that faces the railroad. Just as you approach Main Street you'll be where the ornate Orleans passenger station once stood. Go left onto Main Street and look at the interesting old houses along the way.

14.5 miles: Crossing over Route 6 once again and going downhill to the end, you'll come to the shore at Rock Harbor. Here you can view the Orleans' fleet of fishing boats and dine at Captain Caz's Restaurant.

16.5 miles: Now, you will rejoin the rail-trail and escape the busy streets. The trail shares the right-of-way with power-lines in this area as you travel uphill.

17.3 miles: Grade crossing at Old County Road.

18.2 miles: Another grade crossing, this time at Governor Prence Road.

18.4 miles: Herring Pond is on the left.

18.6 miles: Grade crossing at Samoset Road.

18.8 miles: On your left is Great Pond and on your right is Long Pond.

19.2 miles: Grade crossing at Locust Street. The rail-trail was under construction here in the summer of 1994. In the future it will extend beyond Route 6 to Lecount Hollow Road in South Wellfleet through the Cape Cod National Seashore lands at the Marconi area. The trail extension to be completed in 1995 will be an additional 5 miles.

Bicyclists resting and viewing a cranberry bog on the Cape Cod Rail-Trail

12 Minuteman Bikeway

Endpoints: Loomis Street in Bedford, Massachusetts, to Magnolia Park near the Alewife M.B.T.A. Station in Arlington, Massachusetts.
Location: Middlesex County, Massachusetts. Passing through the towns of Bedford, Lexington, and Arlington, Massachusetts.
Length: 10 Miles
Surface: Asphalt

Uses:

To get there: Take Exit 31B off Rte 95 (128) outside Boston and follow Routes 4 / 225 toward Bedford. Stay on this road for about 2 miles until you come to Loomis Street, which is on the left by a CVS store. Take Loomis Street, go to the end at Railroad Street, and park there.

Contact:
Alan McClennen
Director of Planning and Community Development, Town Hall
730 Massachusetts Avenue
Arlington, MA 02174
617-646-1000 Ext. 4130

Local resources for bike repairs/rentals:
Bikeway Cycle and Sports, 3 Bow Street, Lexington, 617-861-1199.
King Cycle, 198 Great Road, Bedford, 617-275-2035.
Pro-Motion, South Road, Bedford, 617-275-1113
The Bike Stops Here, 43 Dudley Street, Arlington, 617-643-4328.

This trail was built recently (it is 500th in our nation's inventory of reclaimed railroad beds), but it abounds with colonial history. Paul Revere's ride from Boston to Lexington, ahead of advancing British troops, roughly parallels the rail-trail. The trail passes by the Lexington Green, the site of the first battle of the American Revolution.

In 1873 the rail line was formed by the Middlesex Central Railroad. The 1880s saw it absorbed into the Boston & Maine Railroad, where it was known as the Lexington Branch. During World War II, this line boasted tri-weekly freight service, and daily passenger service. Among the passenger trains were two "name trains" (prestigious trains, some with special accommodations), the Paul Revere and the Patriot. The commuter schedule listed five weekday round-trips to Bedford, four of them in the rush-hour time slots. The final passenger train ran in 1977 and the last freight run was in 1981, the year that the line was formally abandoned, but the multi-use path was not finished until 1994.

Although many years in the making, this trail is a testament to proper planning and construction, with thoughtful additions such as mile markers carved from granite and unique motor vehicle barriers built out of cylindrical pipe filled with cement and topped with cast metal bike seats. The barriers stand about four feet high, are painted safety yellow, and need no signage to denote the message of NO MOTOR VEHICLES ALLOWED.

This trail is different from most others because of the wide range of scenery along its journey from rural Bedford to suburban-urban Arlington. The people along the way help to make it special also. On our first trip to this trail in the spring of 1994, we met a kindly, distinguished gentleman, Don Blake, who gave us a tour all the way from Arlington to Bedford. We have found in subsequent trips that acts of kindness are not uncommon on this trail. People are very friendly and helpful to strangers, something special in the 1990s.

Boxed Pony Truss Bridge on Park Avenue in Arlington

12. Minuteman Rail-Trail

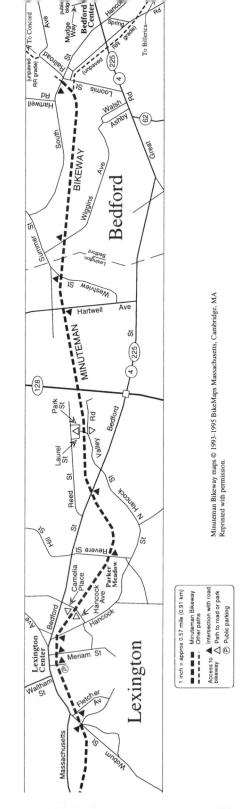

Minuteman Bikeway maps © 1993-1995 BikeMaps Massachusetts, Cambridge, MA
Reprinted with permission.

It's best start in Bedford because parking is easier there. The first thing you will notice when you arrive and look around is that you've entered a mini time-warp so typical of the New England rail-trails. Here in Bedford you will see that an electrical supply business is occupying the former passenger station, a coffee-bakery shop is now in the old freight station, and a bicycle shop is in an old rail-served, lumber-dealer building.

The local historical society has received a grant to study the cost of landscaping the area and painting the railroad buildings in their original B&M cream and maroon scheme. A mock-up of the park is displayed at the Town Hall, and the plan includes a small museum to be located in a Rail-Diesel-Car (RDC)-type commuter passenger car. More information on this project can be obtained by reaching Attorney Jim Shea, 617-275-3212.

There is another historical fact worth noting about Bedford. During the Battle of Lexington and later skirmishes back towards Boston, the only flag carried by the colonial Minutemen was the Bedford Flag. Today this flag is preserved and on display at the Bedford Public Library, about 1/3 mile past the bikeway in the center of town. This is a possible side trip. But now, onto the trail.

0.2 miles: Bridge over a small stream.
1.0 miles: Grade crossing over Wiggins Avenue in Bedford. If you stop and listen, you will hear a rooster proclaim his presence to all the hikers, bicyclists, and roller-bladers.
1.1 miles: Bridge over Shawsheen River.
1.3 miles: Passing through a small forest and a grade crossing at Westview Street in Lexington.
1.5 miles: Grade crossing at Hartwell Avenue, which is busy and has a crossing signal for your convenience.
1.6 miles: Bridge over a small river, where you can see a beaver dam.
1.7 miles: Passing by Topham Swamp from which the Shawsheen River rises. Occasionally, Great Blue Herons can be seen here.
1.8 miles: You are going by a land fill operation for the Town of Lexington. It is now used for leaf recycling.
1.9 miles: Going up-grade now to the bridge over Route 95 / 128.
2.3 miles: Here is an entry point for Valley Road, which runs parallel to the trail at this area.
2.5 miles: School bus company parks their vehicles here.
2.7 miles: Grade crossing over Bedford Street. This is a busy street with quick approaching cars, so be careful.
2.9 miles: The town yard for Lexington is located here on the right.
3.1 miles: Grade crossing for Revere Street. A quiet residential area.

3.3 miles: Entrance to Parker Meadow off to the left as you head east. Also located here is a memorial to Al Lester, a bicyclist who lived in Eastern Mass and rode in the Lexington area regularly. He met a tragic death when struck by a car, while racing in a 24-hour time trial in New York State. His friends in the Charles River Wheelmen, a Boston area cyclist club, erected this small monument in his memory.

3.5 miles: Outlet to Camelia Place.

3.7 miles: Grade crossing at Hancock Street. You nearing the center of Lexington with its history and beautiful antique houses. The Lexington town green, where the battle was fought, is nearby and you might want to take in the Lexington Visitors Center. Open 7 seven days a week (617-862-1450), the Visitors Center offers a wide range of displays and services, including a diorama of the Battle of Lexington Green and historical photos of the ten depots that served this branch of the railroad. Guides to Lexington's extensive conservation lands and bike trails are also available here.

3.9 miles: Grade crossing of Merriam Street.

4.0 miles: Telltale signal is in place here from the days of the steam engine. A telltale is a series of wires hanging from a crossarm above the tracks. These wires would brush against a trainman who might be on the roof, and warn of an approaching tunnel or other restricted vertical clearance area, such as the nearby train-shed, now a bank. The trail goes through the shed area which at one time was the Lexington Railroad Station.

Ex-B & M Lexington Depot, now a bank

LEXINGTON BRANCH

BOSTON—SOMERVILLE JUNCTION, LOWELL & REFORMATORY

Table 51 • 1923

miles	Train Numbers → Stations ↓	3201 A.M.	3205 A.M.	3207 P.M.	3209 P.M.	3211 P.M.	3213 P.M.	3215 P.M.	3217 P.M.	3219 P.M.	3221 P.M.
...	**Boston**	5:35	7:15	§12:20	12:51	3:05	3:48	u4:21	†4:23	u4:40	†4:50
...	East Cambridge	v5:40	......	......	v12:56	......	3:53	......	......	4:35	......
...	Prospect Hill	5:42	......	......	12:58	......	3:55	......	......	4:38	......
...	Winter Hill	5:44	......	......	1:00	......	3:57	......	†4:31	4:40	†4:58
0.0	**Somerville Junction**	5:46	7:25	§12:30	1:02	......	3:59	......	†4:33	4:42	†5:01
0.7	Somerville Highlands	5:48	7:30	......	1:04	......	4:02	......	†4:35	4:45	......
1.1	West Somerville	5:50	7:32	......	1:06	3:15	4:04	......	†4:38	4:48	†5:05
1.6	North Cambridge	5:52	......	......	1:08	3:17	4:06	v4:34	†4:40	4:50	......
2.7	Lake Street	......	......	......	f1:10	......	4:09	......	†4:43	4:54	......
3.5	Arlington	5:57	7:39	§12:36	1:13	3:22	4:12	4:39	......	4:59	†5:12
4.4	Brattle	f6:01	f7:41	§12:39	f1:16	......	f4:16	§4:42	†4:51	|	†5:16
5.2	Arlington Heights	6:04	f7:43	§12:43	1:19	3:27	4:20	§4:44	†4:54	......	†5:20
6.2	East Lexington	f6:06	f7:45	§12:47	f1:22	3:30	f4:23	§4:46	†4:57	......	†5:24
6.9	Pierce's Bridge	f6:08	......	§12:50	f1:24	f3:32	f4:25	§4:48	†4:59	......	†5:27
7.3	Munroe	6:10	f7:48	§12:54	f1:26	3:34	4:27	4:50	......	......	†5:29
8.2	Lexington	6:18	7:52	§12:59	1:31	3:39	4:32	4:55	†5:05	......	†5:34
9.5	North Lexington	f6:21	f7:56	§1:03	f1:35	3:43	e4:37	4:59	|	......	†5:39
12.0	**Bedford**	6:26	8:01	§1:08	1:40	3:48	4:43	5:04	......	......	†5:46

References

f stops to receive or discharge passengers on notice to conductor • **e** stops only to discharge passengers
u no baggage carried • **v** stops only to receive passengers on signal • † except Saturday • § Saturday only •

Lexington Branch schedule from 1923

12 Minuteman Bikeway

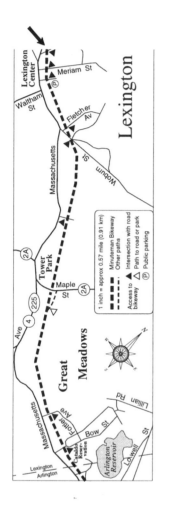

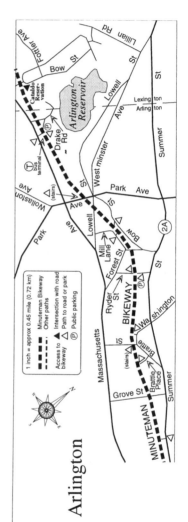

Minuteman Bikeway maps © 1993-1995 BikeMaps Massachusetts, Cambridge, MA
Reprinted with permission.

4.3 miles: Grade crossing over Fletcher Avenue. Look carefully and you'll see an old electrical service mounting for a grade crossing signal unit.

4.4 miles: Hays Lane is intersected here at an oblique angle to give you ample warning of approaching traffic. Note the interesting old VFW post here which is railroad reminiscent.

4.7 miles: Revolutionary era houses nearby.

5.0 miles: The Seasons Four Nursery.

5.4 miles: Maple Street Bridge, a wooden bridge, crosses over the trail at this point. This span has additional support by the insertion of a group of timbers in the center. This area is generally flat and is surrounded by meadows and young trees. Known as the Great Meadows, it is owned by the Town of Arlington, acquired in the last century for water supply purposes.

5.8 miles: Totner Park can be found here with a school on the grounds.

6.3 miles : Grade crossing at Fotler Avenue.

6.4 miles: We start to go downhill now and find ourselves to be riding parallel to Massachusetts Avenue right on the border with Arlington.

6.7 miles: Still going downhill into Arlington proper, following the Mill Brook Valley. A bit of a cut is in this area along with a bridge over the trail.

6.8 miles: Here you can access to Hurd Field. The Arlington Reservoir is found just on the other side of the park. This public area has a mile-long walking path. Swimming in the summer and skating in the winter are some of the activities found here. Mill Brook, which parallels the trail in this area, once powered many mills.

7.0 miles: Here at Arlington Heights is the location of the last active lumber dealer that was on-line. At one time there were five lumberyards, all rail-served between Arlington and Bedford.

7.1 miles: Access to Park Avenue and here also is a wooden truss bridge, known as the "Boxed Pony Truss." This type of bridge was common at one time on the B&M. There are only a handful left in the country today, and two are found together here on this trail. This bridge is a cousin of the picturesque New England covered bridge in that all the load-bearing structural members are enclosed in wood-sheathing, affording a measure of protection from the damaging elements.

7.2 miles: Lowell Street is here with another Boxed Pony Truss bridge. This bridge may be facing replacement in the near future, so you may want to see it before this happens. Also seen here are some examples of rail-served industry that was fairly common on this line in Arlington many years ago. Looking closely, you will see another telltale signal.

7.3 miles: Access to Fraser Road.

7.5 miles: Deck-girder bridge over Arlington Street, a baseball field, and an outlet to Ryder Street.

7.9 miles: Passing by Washington Street access road and an old brick pumping station that was previously coal-fired.

8.1 miles: Brattle Place access is found here.

12. Minuteman Rail-Trail

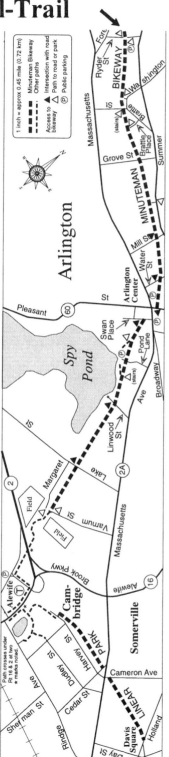

Bikeway Maps
BikeMaps Massachusetts –

Entrepreneur selling lemonade to roller-bladers on the Minuteman Trail

8.2 miles: Thru-Girder bridge is here with impressive stone work abutments.
8.3 miles: We are now passing the Arlington Town Public Works Garage, a former gas works, and Arlington High School with the athletic field in the foreground. This area also might have had a flag stop passenger station. The steps leading up from the school seems to give evidence of this.
8.5 miles: Another mill building, now the home office of Brigham Ice Cream, was rail-served at one time with the loading doors at the trail side.
8.6 miles: Grade crossing of Mill Street.
8.8 miles: Grade Crossing here has two remnants of rail activity, a whistle marker for the engineer to signal his presence and an electrical control cabinet to power the old crossing arms or light standards
9.0 miles: We are now in the streets of Center Arlington. Stay on the sidewalk and follow the signs for the trail. You'll be back on the path shortly.
9.3 miles: Another bridge over a small road, and Spy Pond is on the right. Spy Pond is a beautiful resource of Arlington. Long ago it was used for ice harvesting. Today, if the conditions are right, you will see sailboats and wind surfers. This is another nice area to sit and take in the sights.
9.5 miles: Grade crossing of Linwood Street, another access point to Spy Pond.
10.0 miles: This is the end of the trail proper at Magnolia Park. There are plans to extend the trail to the MBTA Station and towards the Paul Dudley White Trail along the Charles River.

13 City of Northampton Bike Path

Endpoints: Look Park on Route 9, to the north end of State Street, Northampton, Massachusetts.
Location Hampshire County, Northampton, Massachusetts
Length: 2.6 miles
Surface: Asphalt

Uses:

To get there: Start at Look Park, which is on Rt. 9, approximately 2.5 miles northwest of downtown Northampton. The beginning of the Bikeway lies directly across Route 9 at Bridge Road.

Contact:
Wayne Feiden, Principal Planner
Office of Planning and Development
City Hall, 210 Main Street
Northampton, MA 01060
413-586-6950

Local resources for bike repairs/rentals:
F.J. Rogers, 3 Main Street, Florence, MA, 413-584-1727.
Peloton of Northampton, 15 State Street, Northampton, MA, 413-584-1016.
Northampton Bicycle, 319 Pleasant Street, Northampton, MA, 413-586-3810

There are lyrics from a song that say, "I was country, before country was cool." Well, Northampton had a Rail-Trail before Rail-Trails were "cool." This small city in Western Mass. is home to a clean, safe downtown, prestigious Smith College, and a lovely park system. The crown jewel is Look Park. Among the attractions here are paddle boats in a small pond, a miniature train ride, and a small zoo. All reasons in themselves to visit here, but for our purposes it is the convenient place to start the tour of this rail-trail.

This trail began as part of the New York, New Haven, and Hartford Railroad. Until the 1930s there were two parallel railroads that ran through Northampton to the north. The Boston & Maine's (B&M) Connecticut River Division, which runs to this day on the east side of Route 5, and the New Haven which ran basically on the west side of Route 5.

The New Haven Railroad's Canal Branch came up out of Connecticut, entering Massachusetts at Southwick. As it came into Northampton, it joined with the B&M at the beautiful Richardson-designed station, which today is the Depot Restaurant. Both roads then headed north for a short distance and then the NH branched away where the Northampton Honda dealer is currently located. Remains of the footings for the overpass over Route 5 are still visible where the line once headed toward what is now Super Stop & Shop. This commercial development and the others just north of here sit on top of what once was the New Haven's classification yard and engine service facilities, complete with turntable and coaling tower. A branch from this yard led to Williamsburg.

The mainline of the NH's Canal Division ran up to Turners Falls, paralleling the B & M and Route 5. In 1962, the branch was abandoned from the terminus at Williamsburg to Florence, where there was some industry still getting traffic via rail. In 1969, the successor road the infamous Penn-Central abandoned the entire branch all the way back to Route 5.

Today it is known as the Northampton Bikeway. Opened in 1984 as a multi-use path and operated by the City of Northampton, it is a testament to foresight in city planning. There are plans to continue the line to its historic terminus in Williamsburg, though this may not see completion until 1998.

Down-grade approach to Jackson Street overpass.

13. Northampton Bikeway

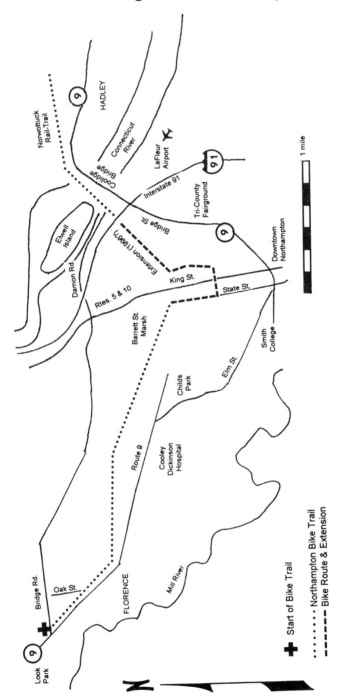

0.0 miles: Use care while crossing Rte 9.

0.2 miles: Here is an impressive fill, and we pass by quiet backyards in the Florence section of Northampton.

0.5 miles: We now cross over Oak Street and pass among some old industrial buildings which are converted to more modern uses and seem to be thriving. This area is near downtown Florence, which is worth a side trip. It is a throwback in time to when things were slower and people were friendlier. It is also the home of the Miss Florence Diner, a genuine chrome diner. Visiting "Miss Flo's" is an unforgettable experience.

1.0 miles: The beginning of the long down-grade to the Rte 5 area.

1.3 miles: Here is another big fill, shortly after which you can see the remains of a spur to the right that at one time served the local industry.

1.6 miles: Construction Services concrete plant is here with its antique loading tower and the remains of a rail siding.

1.7 miles: Look to the right and you will see an old marker that once told the train engineer to blow his whistle as he approached a crossing.

2.2 miles: The down-grade is at its maximum of 2% as we pass under Jackson Street.

2.4 miles On the north side of the trail you'll notice a gravel and trap-rock path which leads to the Barrett Street Marsh Conservation Area, with its rich wetlands complex. Definitely worth viewing for the varied bird-life.

2.6 miles: The improved trail ends here at the north end of State Street. Directly ahead is an old 40-foot boxcar used for storage at Acme Auto Body.

There are some plans in place to join the Northampton Bikeway and the Norwottuck Rail-Trail, which are presently about one mile apart. This section will be constructed as a bike route, and not as a rail-trail. This logical extension should be completed in 1996.

14 Norwottuck Rail-Trail

Endpoints: Elwell State Park, Damon Road, Northampton, Massachusetts to Station Road, Amherst, Massachusetts.
Location: Hampshire County, Massachusetts towns of Northampton, Hadley, and Amherst.
Length: 9 miles
Surface: Asphalt

Uses:

To get there: Damon Road is located just off Interstate 91 North at exit 19. At the foot of the ramp go straight through the light. Take the first driveway into Elwell State Park. There is ample parking.

Contact:
Daniel O'Brien, Bikeway and Trail Planner
Department of Environmental Management
100 Cambridge Street Room 1404
Boston, MA 02202
617-727-3160 Ext. 557

Local resources for bike repairs/rentals:
Bicycle World Too, 63 S. Pleasant Street, Amherst, 413-253-7722
Competitive Edge, 374 Russell Street (Rte. 9), Hadley, 413-585-8833
Peloton of Northampton, 15 State Street, Northampton, 413-584-1016
Northampton Bicycle 319 Pleasant Street, Northampton, 413-586-3810
F.J. Rogers, 3 Main Street, Florence, 413-584-1727
Valley Bicycles, 319 Main Street, Amherst, 413-256-0880

This Rail-trail is the newest one in Massachusetts, having been completed in 1993. It has many interesting historical and recreational aspects. The railroad line on which the bikeway runs was originally owned by the Central Massachusetts Railroad. Completed in 1887, it was envisioned as a third route to Boston, one without the excessive grades and curves of the competing Boston & Albany Railroad (B&A) and the Fitchburg Railroad (predecessor of the Boston & Maine Railroad).

The line was eventually swallowed up by the Boston & Maine (B&M) and relegated to secondary status. It did, however, have daily passenger service to Boston until 1932, when the depression cut into the level of business. A dearth of on-line industry slowly cut freight traffic levels until the mid 1970s, when the local out of Northampton ran only once a week as an "extra." By this time, the track speed was down to ten mph or less due to the "deferred maintenance" of the track. The federal law stating a 12-hour maximum for a train crew to be on duty made it almost impossible for a round trip from Northampton to Ware, Massachusetts, which was as far as the line went by this time.

In 1980 the line from Northampton to Norwottuck Junction was formally abandoned in a petition with the Interstate Commerce Commission. In the mid-80s the idea of a bikeway began to be discussed. After some fits and starts due to funding problems, it was finally opened in the summer of 1993. It is managed as a linear park by the Massachusetts Dept. of Environmental Management. The trail has some features that are extraordinary. Foremost is the bridge over the Connecticut River, a truss bridge of 1,400 feet and 7 spans long. This was the longest crossing on this river for the B&M, undoubtedly a cause of headaches at the their operations department because weight restrictions prohibited all but the smallest locomotives from running over it. Today, however, the bridge is useful once again, for it marks the start of the rail-trail.

Bridge over the Connecticut River

14. Norwottuck Rail-Trail

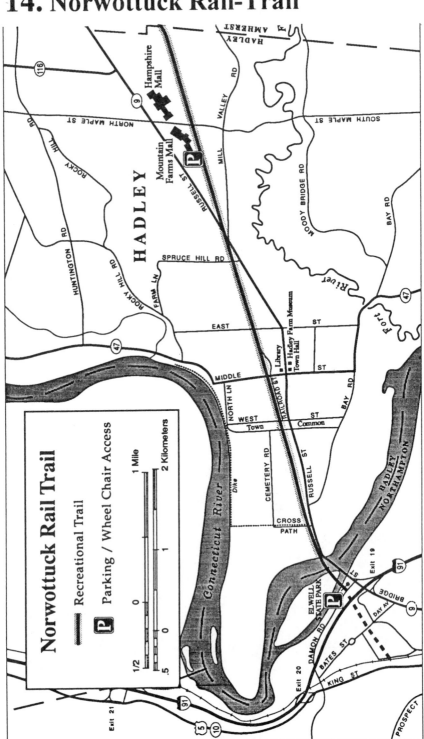

Norwottuck Rail Trail

Recreational Trail

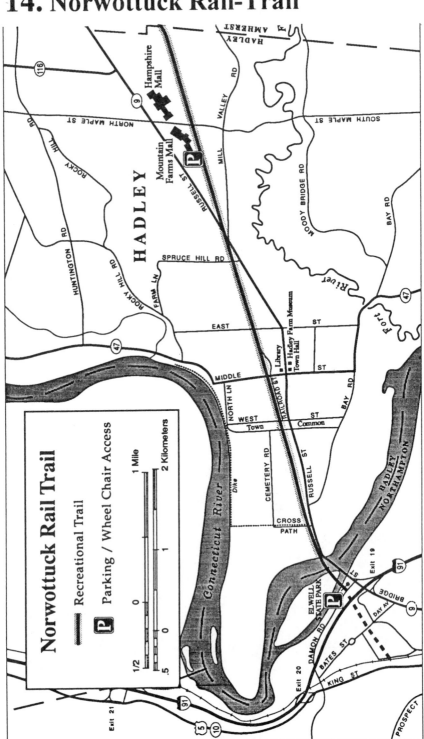 Parking / Wheel Chair Access

0.0 miles: As you head onto the bridge, you will notice Calvin Coolidge Bridge to the south, named for the Northampton resident who became president. This carries Rte 9, which will run parallel to the trail for much of the journey. If you look at the shore under the bridge on the Northampton side, you'll see a dock. This is primarily used by local colleges to launch their racing shells which are seen in the late spring on the river.

0.1 miles: Looking out over the majestic Connecticut River, you'll see Elwell Island, namesake for the park. Bring your binoculars and you can observe birds that are not normally seen in suburban backyards. Many types of water fowl from sea gulls to herons can be seen here. Eagles and various hawks ride the updrafts searching for their prey. Over 150 species of birds have been identified along the river, many of them using the Connecticut River as their path for migration. The Holyoke Range is visible to the south. If you tour this way in the summer months, you will also see an abundance of pleasure craft. In the late 19th century the Connecticut River was known as the nation's best landscaped sewer. That is not the case anymore, as millions of dollars have been spent to clean up this resource. It is once again the jewel of the Pioneer Valley.

0.3 miles: Grade crossing of Cross-Path Road.

0.8 miles: A small culvert passes under the trail here.

1.7 miles: Grade Crossing of West Street in the area of the Hadley Green. Here you will come upon an old abandoned freight house and side track area. This little depot is reminiscent of B&M architecture of the late nineteenth century. It is sitting undisturbed as a reminder of simpler and slower times. Just ahead you will find another forgotten token of the past, the small town coal and lumber dealer, complete with a genuine "Blue Anthracite Coal" sign. You will also see an antique coal elevator used to transfer coal to a truck.

View of the Holyoke Range from the Norwottuck Trail.

14 Norwottuck Rail-Trail

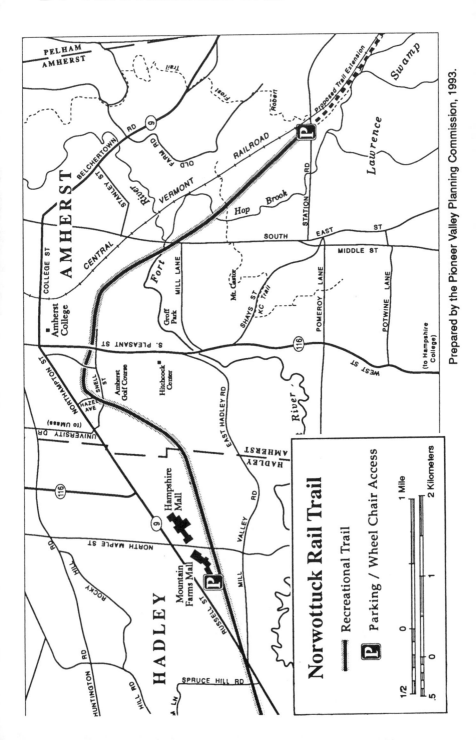

Prepared by the Pioneer Valley Planning Commission, 1993.

Norwottuck Rail Trail

Recreational Trail

🅿 Parking / Wheel Chair Access

B & M Railroad Station, Amherst, circa 1915. Today it is a part of Amherst Farmers Supply complex viewable from the Norwottuck Trail [courtesy of Richard Symmes, Walker Transportation Collection of the Beverly Historical Society]

1.9 miles: Grade crossing of Middle Street. Hadley Town Hall and Library are nearby.

2.3 miles: Grade crossing for East Street. An old rail-served industry here has been converted to more modern uses.

2.8 miles: Spruce Hill Road passes overhead as the trail goes into a tunnel.

3.3 miles: Under busy Route 9 is the tunnel which was the major expense in the conversion to a rail-trail.. This was once an unprotected grade crossing.

3.4 miles: Pete's Drive-Inn, a handy place to get a soda or lunch, borrow a wrench, or just rest and chat with fellow travelers. In the summer of 1994 Pete added car-hops to serve food and drinks to people's cars. This is just a fun place to go, whether on a bike or with your family in the evening.

4.1 miles: Mountain Farms Mall, with parking close to the trail. This is an alternate parking lot (instead of Elwell State Park). If you are interested in selecting something healthy for the remainder of the trip, a natural food store called Bread and Circus is located in this complex.

4.2 miles: Grade Crossing for South Maple Street, Hampshire Mall on the left.

5.2 miles: Hickory Ridge Country Club will now be on your right as you go through a heavily forested section.

5.7 miles: Bridge over Snell Street. A Christmas Tree Farm is here.

Bridge over the Fort River, Amherst, Massachusetts.

5.9 miles: Overhead is the Woodside Avenue Bridge which is open only to pedestrians. It has been closed to vehicles for many years.

6.0 miles: You are now riding next to the Amherst College Football Field, and the biggest cut on the trail. This is a peaceful section, with its dark shadows, ground covers, and evergreen scents. Look carefully and you'll see some old track lying off to the side, one of the few hints that this was at one time a railroad.

6.2 miles: Rte 116 will pass overhead, and then you are at Amherst Farmers Supply. One of their buildings is the old Amherst Passenger Station circa 1900, where they currently store some of their inventory. Note the semaphore signal, which is still in good overall condition, and the bay window for the dispatcher to sit and watch the approaching trains. Amherst center is only 1/2 mile west of here on Rte 116. This is a nice place to visit with its many shops and stores.

7.5 miles: You are now approaching the twin bridges area. The first is a Deck Truss design over the Fort River. The second is a thru-girder type over South East Street. If time permits, you could go below onto the road to view these structures from the ground. There is an outlet to the road below just east of the second bridge. Be careful because the traffic is deceptive. As you gaze up at the right-of-way, try to visualize a steam-powered passenger train pounding across this bridge at 40 mph. It is amazing that bridges like these supported such weight. If time still permits, you can soak your feet in the cool Fort River.

7.9 miles: This section has one of the many nature walks in Amherst. This particular one goes through the Lawrence Swamp. Bring your binoculars because the bird life is varied and bountiful.

9.0 miles: The trail ends at Station Road in Amherst, where you will find a parking lot. The Station Road area is near another one of Amherst's walking trails; the Robert Frost Trail. It runs 36 miles, and can be accessed at this end of the Norwottuck Trail. Look across the street and you will see where the original rail bed continues. It leads to the spot where Norwottuck Junction once stood, approximately 1/2 mile further on. This connection with the Central Vermont Railway was made in 1941, when the B&M abandoned the 8.5 mile stretch to Canal Junction in Belchertown. Planning is in the works to extend the rail-trail beyond the current terminus. The 1.7-mile addition would end at Warren Wright Road in Belchertown.

B & M (left) and Central Vermont (right) trains at Norwottuck Junction, 1947
Contemporary view of this area is seen on page 13.
[Don Robinson photo from the Walker Transportation Collection of the Beverly Historical Society]

15 Falmouth Shining Sea Trail

Endpoints: Locust Street, Falmouth, Massachusetts to Steamship Authority Dock, Woods Hole, Massachusetts
Location: Barnstable County, Falmouth, and Woods Hole Massachusetts,
Length: 3.2 miles
Surface: Asphalt

Uses:

To get there: The best place to start is where it is most convenient to park, which is in Falmouth. Parking is available throughout the town at metered areas and at the town lot located at the start of the trail on Locust Street.
Contact:
Kevin Lynch, Chairman, Falmouth Bikeway Committee
Town Hall, Falmouth, Massachusetts 02540
508-548-7611
Local resources for bike repairs/rentals:
Corner Cycle, 115 Palmer Avenue, Falmouth, 508-540-4195.
Holiday Cycle, 465 Grand Avenue, Falmouth, 508-540-3549.

Shining Sea Trail curving along the shore.

Signage along the way

This is one of two trails located on Cape Cod. Though only slightly longer than three miles, it is the equal of the twenty plus mile Cape Cod Rail-Trail in terms of scenic beauty and interesting sights along the way.

We begin in Falmouth which is the part of the Cape which is best described as being closest to the "shoulder." Falmouth is off the main Cape highway and is not as crowded with tourists as are other towns along the Cape. The railroad was completed here in 1872 and was used primarily as a passenger line to bring tourists to the steamship terminal at Woods Hole. From there they went to Martha's Vineyard and Nantucket. Rail service ended with the coming of the automobile and construction of the modern highways to the Cape. The New Haven Railroad ended passenger service in 1959 and discontinued all service in 1964, while the official abandonment (as filed with the Interstate Commerce Commission) did not take place until 1968, and it wasn't converted to a multi-use path until 1975.

"Shining Sea" was named in memory of Katherine Lee Bates, a resident who wrote "America the Beautiful." This is a trail for the whole family, from young to old. Because of its short distance, no one will get tired and the scenic beauty packed in the small package will not let anyone get bored. You will pass salt marshes, deserted beaches, fresh water ponds, and picturesque New England harbors. The trail has some splendid views of Martha's Vineyard, located seven miles off-shore, and it also passes by Nobska Lighthouse, which many will recognize from calendar pictures of New England.

15. Shining Sea Trail

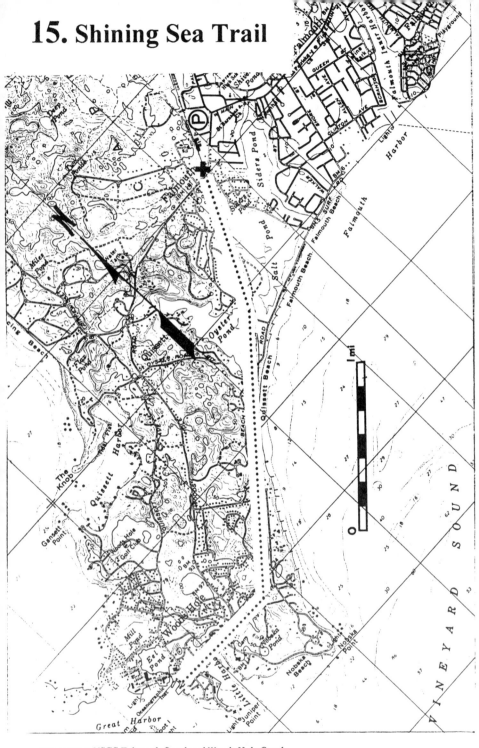

map source: USGS Falmouth Quad and Woods Hole Quad

0.0 miles: Starting at the Locust Street Parking Lot, this is where a railroad crossing tender's house once stood.

0.3 miles: Black Locust trees are found here along with a some honeysuckle.

0.5 miles: Salt Pond is here, along with benches. Salt Pond is a glacial kettle hole formed when the last Ice Age receded approximately 12,000 years ago.

0.9 miles: Elm Road Crossing.

1.0 miles: A fill was constructed here to allow the railroad to pass alongside a pond. This was done in the days before environmental impact studies were mandated, and the fill has restricted the flow of water from one side to the next. This area has ancient ties and rail, one of the few signs of its railroad heritage.

1.1 miles: Oyster Pond is here, along with some benches. The oysters disappeared in the late 18th century when a sand bar developed across the mouth, cutting off the flow of salt water. The swans you see here are Trumpeter Swans. Year-round residents, they are among the most graceful of birds.

1.2 miles: Natural cranberries are found here where the water table is exposed in shallow marshes. Here also can be found one of the few remaining signs of a railroad on this trail. A stone marker with a "W" inscribed was used to let the engineer known to sound the whistle because there is a crossing coming up. This is Surf Drive Crossing, where you can go on the beach facing Vineyard Sound and relax, follow the road to Falmouth, or continue on the trail.

1.4 miles: Trunk River Bridge. During the spring a herring run goes under here into Oyster Pond.

1.6 miles: This is O'Hara Pond, a fresh water pond, where you can find some benches. To the north you can see some of the research laboratories of Woods Hole Oceanographic Institute.

1.7 miles: A view of the Woods Hole Oceanographic Coastal Lab and Dock.

1.9 miles: Fay Road Bridge

2.2 miles: A stone marker indicates it is 71 miles from South Station in Boston. From 1884 to 1916 the "Dude" train made the run from Boston to Woods Hole in 1 hour and 48 minutes.

2.4 miles: Stone foundation marks the site of a windmill that pumped water from the swamp to a basin on the other side of the hill. It was then used to replenish the water in the steam locomotive.

2.6 miles: Nobska Road Overpass. Railroad Pond is south of the bridge.

2.8 miles: This is Little Harbor, where the Coast Guard maintains navigational buoys. You can see Martha's Vineyard in the distance, and the first of the Elizabeth Islands chain, Naushon Island.

2.9 miles: This stone dock was the original ferry dock during the 18th century.

3.1 miles: Railroad Avenue Underpass. This area is also the parking lot for the Steamship Authority, which runs the ferry service to the Islands.

3.2 miles: The end of the line. The New Haven once had an Armstrong turntable here on the waters edge to turn steam locomotives around by hand. The term "Armstrong" came into being from the effort required to turn the engine. There are many fine places here to view the harbor. Enjoy.

Future Rail-Trails in Massachusetts

The following information was provided by Doug Mink of the Bicycle Coalition of Massachusetts, P.O. Box 1015, Cambridge MA 02142, (617)-491-RIDE.

Boston Metropolitan Area

Neponset River Bikepath

The MDC-owned right-of-way, ex-New Haven Old Colony Division, extends from the harbor in Dorchester to Central Street in Milton on the south bank of the Neponset River, giving access to the marshes as well as connecting with the MDC's harbor path. The Boston Natural Areas Fund is considering extending this path up the Neponset to Readville, where a side spur could easily connect to the Blue Hills, though bike lanes on parkways might be necessary.

Bike to the Sea

A group of cyclists in Malden thought up this rail-with-trail bikepath from the center of Malden through Everett to Revere Beach. A preliminary study is being conducted in 1995.

Minuteman Bikeway Extension

The right-of-way used by the Minuteman Commuter Bikeway continues westward through Bedford and Concord to Acton. Another branch off of this line runs from Bedford to Billerica. The problems facing this project include crossing the Assabet River, where the bridge has been removed, and Route 2 (near the West Concord rotary). The Concord-Acton branch would connect with the Lowell Sudbury trail.

Central Massachusetts Trail

The MBTA owns the Waltham to Hudson section of this unused rail right-of-way, known as the Central Massachusetts Division of the Boston & Maine Railroad, which once ran from Waltham to Northampton. Preliminary studies have been performed. The line west of Hudson, while in private hands, is mostly undeveloped and may be recoverable. There is a wonderful 1/4 mile tunnel in Clinton right above the Wachusett Reservoir Dam which could be the terminus of a 40-mile long trail from Boston, running parallel to Route 20 through Waltham, Weston, Wayland, and Sudbury, then through Hudson and Berlin to Clinton. After the reservoir, the right-of-way continues across the middle of the state to the Quabbin Reservoir, which now has to be detoured, to Amherst, where the Norwottuck Trail follows it to Northampton. The Waltham City Planning department is taking the lead on developing this trail.

Assabet River Rail-Trail

A group of citizens is working to establish a 12-mile bike and pedestrian path on a long abandoned B&M right-of-way paralleling the Assabet River from Hudson to Maynard, with connections to Marlborough and South Acton.

Lowell-Sudbury Trail

It has been proposed that part of the mostly unused Old Colony (ex-New Haven Railroad) line from Framingham to Lowell be converted to a Sudbury-to-Lowell bicycle-horse path. Running through Sudbury, Concord, Acton, Westford, and Chelmsford, it would connect the Minuteman Bikeway Extension in Acton and the Central Massachusetts Bikepath in Sudbury. A preliminary study was performed by the state Central Transportation Planning Staff, and though some public hearings have been held, the project has been on hold for years.

Central and Western Massachusetts

Southern New England Trunkline

This railroad was planned but never quite finished because its chief proponent went down with the Titanic in 1912. Today, part of this line is a 20-mile-long multiple-use, unpaved trail which runs between the Franklin and Douglas State Forests. It connects to other trails in Connecticut and Rhode Island and is recognized as a National Recreational Trail. It is owned and maintained by the Department of Environmental Management.

Quinebaug Valley Trail

This 10.8-mile-long trail on the former Providence and Worcester Railroad (ex-New Haven Railroad) Southbridge Branch links Southbridge, Dudley, and Webster, Massachusetts, as well as Thompson, Connecticut. The Grand Trunk Trail Blazers are the volunteers here.

Ashuwillticook River Trail

Running 17.5 miles from Pittsfield to North Adams along Rte 8 and the Hoosic River, this ex-New Haven Railroad Berkshire Division line is an excellent candidate for a north-south path in the Berkshires.

Great Rail-Trails of New Hampshire

16. **Mason Rail-Trail**
17. **Rockingham Recreational Trail**
18. **Sugar River Recreational Trail**
19. **Wolfeboro/Sanbornville**
     Recreational Trail

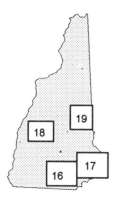

Rock quarry along the Mason Rail-Trail

The four Rail-Trails that are included in this section are all slightly different in surroundings and purpose. They do share one common trait; they were all at one time or another owned by the Boston & Maine Railroad, whose route map in this state was a study in redundant trackage and backwoods ramblings. 1995 will see the state acquire and develop more old B&M rights-of-way.

The Wolfeboro line was primarily a tourist line with a connection to Lake Winnipesaukee resorts via a steam-ship. Eventually, the lack of freight traffic caused it to be sold to a shortline entrepreneur who ran a modestly successful tourist passenger operation, but the continuing lack of freight caused the line to be abandoned. Today this Rail-Trail has two personalities; one a conventional crushed gravel trail that goes by a picturesque lake and the other, a rail-in-place park with a shoulder for hikers and single track riding.

The Mason Rail-Trail is for those who are seeking solitude and an interesting view of a southern New Hampshire valley. This branch of the B&M was for many years one of the most obscure, particularly after the nearby quarry closed and traffic dwindled to a minimum.

The Sugar River Trail is for those who love bridges and an accompanying river for the length of the trip. Two of the country's few remaining railroad covered bridges are included, along with a good sense of being on a railroad. Some trails, when in the process of upgrading from "rails"-to-"trails," get sterilized and stripped of all history. The Sugar River Trail still displays a few pieces of archaeology along the way to give you a few surprises.

The Rockingham Recreational Trail is a little unusual because it is set up primarily for ATVs. Other modes are welcome but you are advised that motorized traffic will be encountered. This should not be a deterrent because the ATV operators are almost always courteous and careful not to scare or otherwise disturb hikers or bicyclists.

16 Mason Railroad Trail

Endpoints: Route 123 in West Townsend, Massachusetts at the border with Mason, New Hampshire to Mason, New Hampshire.
Location: Hillsborough County, Mason, New Hampshire.
Length: 9.2 miles
Surface: Gravel and original ballast

Uses:

To get there: Out of Fitchburg, Massachusetts, take Route 13 north, to Route 124 west, to Route 123, about 12 miles altogether. While on Route 123, the border with New Hampshire will be marked by a small granite obelisk. Here is also a small gravel parking area. Park here and bike or hike approximately 200 yards north to Morse Road. Take a right onto Morse Road; follow it to the top of the hill. The Mason Trail bisects this street. Go left and enjoy the trail.
Contact:
Liz Fletcher
Mason Conservation Commission
Mann House
Mason, NH 03048
603-878-2070
Local resources for bike repairs/rentals:
Happy Day Cycle, 237 South Street Milford, NH, 603-673-5088.
Absolutely Bicycles, North Road, New Ipswitch, NH, 603-878-4059.

This is a perfect example of a general rule about rail-trails: they are often built in areas that the original railroad had to abandon due to a lack of population or lack of an industry that is readily rail-served. This is one of those obscure Boston and Maine Railroad branch lines that went into the woods off the main line and disappeared for miles.

This branch started out as the Peterboro and Shirley Railroad in the mid-1800s. With its connection to the main line at Ayer, Massachusetts, it was destined to be a shortcut to Vermont. Unfortunately, declining business fortunes meant it was never to be finished beyond Greenville, New Hampshire. At one time, the branch was fairly busy with on-line granite quarries and a grain mill in the town of Greenville.

In the 1950s, the local freighter came up out of Ayer six days a week. By the sixties, the traffic had dried up enough to warrant only twice-weekly service. B&M management had the line north of West Townsend, Massachusetts embargoed (self abandoned) in 1973. The end came with the ICC approving the formal abandonment in 1979.

This trail has a special rural touch, and you are likely not to find another soul on its quiet path. If it's solitude you're looking for, you've found it. Let's begin.

Approaches to bridge over Black Brook.

16. Mason Railroad Trail

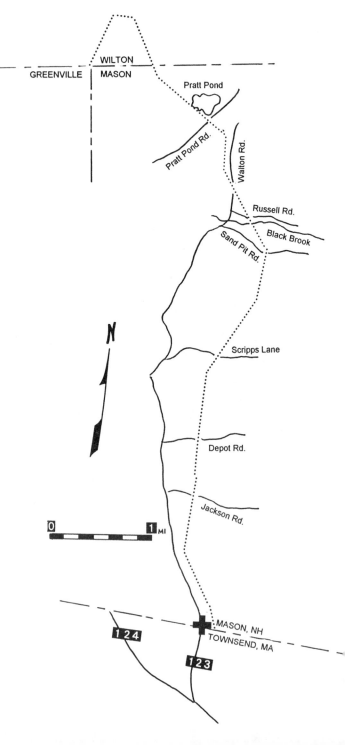

0.0 mile: At the intersection with Morse Road you will notice a small stream and its waterfall -- a peaceful start to this peaceful trail.

0.4 mile: An interesting rock cut with various kinds of moss growing on the rocks and leftover ties. As you travel on the cinder bed, you will notice a 10-to-15-degree drop in temperature in this moist glade.

0.5 miles: A granite whistle marker, obviously of B&M heritage, stands here as a lonely marker of the past. Also in this area is a fill of respectable size with the west side 25 feet lower than the trail.

1.0 mile: Another rock cut with the ferns and moss characteristic of this area.

1.2 miles: Slight uphill with a marsh on the right.

1.5 miles: Rock cut again.

1.7 miles: Wooden deck bridge over Jackson Road.

2.2 miles: Depot Road. No sign of a depot anymore; however, the trail does widen up considerably in this area as you continue north.

2.8 miles: The trail is still wide and generally uphill. There is a stone wall on each side of the trail here that was probably built over 150 years ago.

3.2 miles: You cross over Scripps Lane.

3.4 miles: Signs are evident of a granite operation with tailings piles and unfinished blocks haphazardly tossed about.

4.0 miles: Rock cut with a slow-moving and mucky stream on each side.

4.4 miles: Grade crossing for Sand Pit Road.

4.8 miles: You are now coming upon a narrow bridge over the Black Brook. The approach to this bridge is relatively steep for a rail-trail, and the bridge itself is narrow, so be careful.

4.9 miles: Grade crossing for Russell Road.

5.1 miles: On a fill again with a marsh on either side.

5.2 miles: Walton Road grade crossing.

5.5 miles: The road to the right and below is Walton Road. You are on a fill.

5.6 mile: You're in open country now as you pass under some power transmission lines and then back into the woods.

6.1 miles: Grade crossing of Pratt Pond Road. Pratt Pond will be upon you quickly. This is a good place to rest and watch the frogs compete with the dragon flies for the mosquitoes.

6.8 miles: Back into dense forest again.

7.2 miles: Out of the woods and under some power transmission lines again. Off to the right, looking "down the line," you can see clear across a valley that you couldn't previously know was there.

7.7 miles: Going uphill again as you are on a bit of a fill. The trail gets narrow in this area as the trees are encroaching on the right-of-way.

8.0 miles: Now we are on the biggest fill of the trail, 35-40-foot drops on each side, but only about 1/10 mile in length.

Piers are all that remain of the bridge to Greenville.

8.3 miles: Granite cut in this area. Look for the evidence of hand cutting of the rocks. Just on the other side of the cut is a patch of mountain laurel which blooms with beautiful white flowers in late June.

8.8 miles: Another fill with a steep drop to the right.

9.0 miles: Crossing a paved road. The trail continues on the other side, but it is a bit of a challenge with the berm of dirt placed there. This is to prevent cars from getting onto the trail.

9.1 miles: Another rock cut is found here along with a 10-to-15-degree temperature difference. This cut is long at 1/10 mile, which explains the cooler temperatures.

9.2 miles: This is the end of the trail, and you'll think it was worth the effort when you see the piers for the trestle that once crossed this valley. They are over 60 feet in height. Mountain climbers practice here sometimes with all their gear and lines. The other side of the valley is the town of Greenville, which once had an active grain mill and a passenger station. Both of these structures still stand and the passenger station is undergoing a restoration.

Greenville, New Hampshire passenger station

17 Rockingham Recreational Trail

Endpoints: Windham Depot Road, Windham, New Hampshire to Rte 107 Fremont, New Hampshire. Extension runs from Freemont, to Epping, New Hampshire.
Location: Rockingham County, New Hampshire. Passing through the towns of Windham, Derry, Hampstead, Sandown, Freemont, and Epping.
Length: 14.2 miles and a 4-mile non-motorized vehicle extension.
Surface: Sand, gravel, and original ballast. Soft in some areas and washboard in others. (Washboarded areas are graded out twice-a-year.)

Uses:

To get there: Take I-93 to exit 4, then Rte 102 northeast to Rte 28 south. Take a right onto Windham Depot Road and in about 1.5 miles you'll see a depot building on left. Park here.
Contact:
Paul Gray, Chief, Department of Trails
New Hampshire Department of resources and Economic Development
P.O. Box 856, Concord, NH 03302
603-271-3254
Local resources for bike repairs/rentals:
Bike Barn, Too, 14 East Broadway, Derry, 603-432-7907.
Cycles Etceteras, 13 Range Road, Salem, 603-890-3212.
Flyin Wheels, 450 South Broadway, Salem, 603-893-0225.
Merrimack Bicycle Shop, 1 Pinkerton Street, Derry, 603-437-0277.

This is another one of those ubiquitous branch lines of the old B&M Railroad that in the final years went nowhere important. The early years, however, were a different story altogether. The original purpose of this line was to connect the burgeoning city of Worcester, Massachusetts, with the town of Nashua, New Hampshire, and Portland, Maine, and points beyond. This was done by two railroad companies, the Portland & Rochester, and the Worcester, Nashua & Rochester. The two entities which comprised the route were absorbed into the Boston & Maine Railroad, by way of the old Eastern Railroad, in 1886. It then became known as the Worcester, Nashua & Portland Division of the Boston & Maine Railroad. At the turn of the century, two passenger through-trains ran on this line, carrying people to Maine connections and onward to the Canadian Maritimes. This line handled the largest volume of freight traffic of any un-signaled single-line track in the country.

The majority of the traffic, however, was in the southern section of the line, up to Nashua. By the early 1930s, traffic continued to deteriorate to the point that the B&M petitioned the Interstate Commerce Commission for permission to abandon the section between Hudson and Freemont, New Hampshire, in 1934. The petition was granted and the tracks were pulled out in 1935.

In the mid-1980s, the state of New Hampshire made the right-of-way a multi-use path, with a focus on the blossoming popularity of ATVs, dirt bikes, and snowmobiles. Though hikers and mountain bikes are welcome, it should be noted that this trail will have significant motorized traffic. A 4-mile extension to Epping, New Hampshire, has been included in the trail description here. This section is owned by the state, but is not part of the portion open to the ATV-type vehicles. This is because of the close proximity to neighboring houses. --- Please!! No motor vehicles on the extension.

Gentleman farmer's meadow and pond on the trail in Derry.

17. Rockingham Recreational Trail

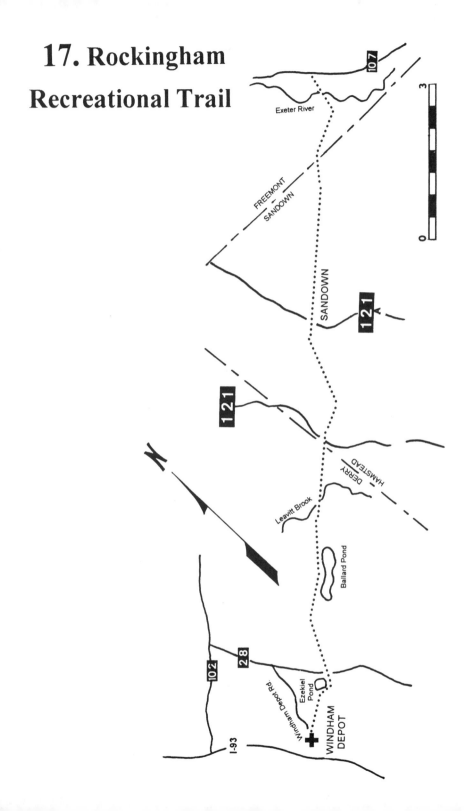

0.0 miles: At the start, you'll see the Windham Depot, an old B & M style depot with its usual steep roof lines. This complex today is used as the highway department's salt and sand storage area. As you go to the rear of the depot, you'll see the remains of two rail beds. Take the left one to start the trip. The trail is fairly wide and well kept. The surface here is dirt, but not too soft for riding.

0.2 miles: The parallel trail is starting to diverge to the south because a ravine, which is over 50 feet in some places, comes between the two branches.

0.4 miles: Still in the woods. A stone foundation is on the left and an old stone bridge that crossed a now dried-up stream.

0.6 miles: A small cut is found here with some cut stone blocks used to reinforce the hill.

0.7 miles: On a fill here with gentle sides, some houses are nearby and a dirt road crossing the trail.

0.8 miles: Grade crossing of a driveway.

1.0 miles: Grade crossing of Windham Depot Road.

1.1 miles: Ezekiel Pond is now visible on the left. You are now between the pond and the Windham Depot Road.

1.2 miles: As you come upon the intersection of Route 28, you'll see a huge, partially completed house, a testament to the over-building of the 1980s. Today it is forlorn and abandoned, exposed to the elements through the broken windows. As you cross the highway be careful as the cars fly by.

1.4 miles: Grade crossing of Stark Road.

1.6-1.9 miles: Soft ground here with a sand base. A marsh area is on each side of the trail.

2.0 miles: A small pond is on the right.

2.1 miles: More standing water is found here on the left.

2.3 miles: Grade crossing of a dirt road.

2.4 miles: On a fill that is fairly high at 20 feet.

2.6 miles: Going past a pond that has a meadow and a typical New Hampshire farmhouse. A perfect place to rest and take in the view.

2.7 miles: An agricultural grade crossing that accesses the meadow you've just passed. After a storm, it can be muddy here.

2.8 miles: A grade crossing of Island Gulf Road.

3.1-3.4 miles: Ballard Pond is on the right and about 20 feet below.

4.0 miles: Grade crossing at Warner Hill Road.

4.2 miles: Power lines pass overhead as the trail widens.

4.4 miles: On a small fill as the woods encroach upon you once again.

4.8 miles: Once again another fill and pond on each side. This scene is a graphic reason why these rail-trails are so valuable. Today it would be virtually impossible to fill in the middle of a lake for any reason. But here you are, dry and yet in the middle a of pond, able to view birds or other creatures that are normally not easily visible from the distant shore.

5.1 miles: On another small fill that carries you over more wetlands. New housing on the left is more evidence of the boom 80s here in southern New Hampshire.

5.3 miles: Steep down-grade and then a sharp up-grade. It is obvious that a bridge used to be here, but was taken out. Marshes on each side here are fed by Leavitt Brook and Drew Brook.

5.5 miles: Out of the swampy areas and into a deeply forested cut.

5.8 miles: Going past another marsh area.

6.2 miles: Trail gets wide in this area and there seems to be evidence of previous railroad activity such as a small yard or servicing facility just to the west of Rte 121, on the Hampstead line. Rte 121 is crossed by climbing up to the highway. New construction has raised the level of the road. On the other side of the road it may be wet, particularly after a storm.

6.5 miles: You will be coming upon a fork in the trail, bear left to continue.

6.6 miles: Going past an ancient stone wall.

6.9 miles: On a fill going past more marshes.

7.1 miles: Grade crossing at Kent Farm Road, which is near the Hampstead-Sandown border.

7.5 miles: Now on a fill above the forest floor. Some cribbing is here to facilitate a culvert.

Restored station at Sandown, New Hampshire

7.8 miles: Grade crossing.

7.9 miles: Grade crossing of a dirt road and into the biggest cut thus far. It may be wet here.

8.2-8.4 miles: You are now on the biggest fill. This one is about 50 feet tall.

8.5 miles: A concrete culvert and the trail tends to bend to the right.

8.7 miles: Grade crossing and a neighboring small pond on the left.

9.0 miles: This is Sandown Station. Located at Route 121A in Sandown, it is an authentic Worcester, Nashua, and Portland Railroad Company passenger station. This interesting structure was built in 1873 and handled a lot of traffic up until the end of scheduled service in 1933. A "name train," the Bar-Harbor Express, ran this way carrying such people as the Roosevelts and the Rockefellers to their summer "cottages" on the coast of Maine. Today this is the home of the Sandown Historical Society and they pride themselves on their fine job of restoration. It is usually staffed in the summer months on Sunday afternoons and has a variety of exhibits inside and out depicting life in general, and railroading in particular, at the turn of the century. It makes for a highlight of the trip to stop here and chat with the volunteers or just browse.

9.5 miles: A pond is on each side.

9.7 miles: Cinder surface with a pond on the right and a swamp on the left.

10.0 miles: A cut is here, and the forest is dense in this area

10.3 miles: On a fill again. This one is about 20 feet high.

10.8 miles: Grade crossing of a road where the Sandown Materials Company is located, a supplier of gravel.

10.9 miles: A cinder ballasted fill.

11.0 miles: Wooden ridge over a small stream.

11.3 miles: Concrete culvert bridge.

11.7 miles: Passing under three sets of high tension wires.

11.9 miles: Grade crossing of a road.

12.2 miles: Bridge over a small stream.

12.3 miles: Wide open swamps on each side of the road-bed.

12.6 miles: Into the forest again, but the trail has a firmer and smoother surface. This is the Fremont town line area.

12.8 miles: Swamps on the right and a dead forest are visible here.

13.3 miles: Grade crossing at South Road, which used to cross the railroad via a bridge. Today you must go up a steep embankment and down again to rejoin the trail.

13.8 miles: Through girder type bridge crossing the Exeter River.

14.0 miles: Swamps again on the left and a small up-grade on the right.

14.2 miles: This is the east end of the trail, at a parking lot in Freemont, at Route 107. A convenience store can be found nearby by taking a right onto 107 and going a short distance The Freemont Passenger Station is across the street and today is used as a private residence.

Extension

0.0 miles: As you cross the road and start, please do not trespass on the land of the owner of the Freemont station. It will be obvious where the right of way goes, but do not disturb the people who live here.

0.1 miles: A marsh and some old ties are seen here. A passing siding was in place here years ago. This was probably installed to get passenger trains around the local way-freights that were working in the area.

0.2 miles: A gate is here to prevent trespassing by cars or other vehicles.

0.6 miles: Now you're in a small cut with gentle sloping sides as the woods thicken and surround the trail. A grade crossing of a dirt road is here. This is probably a fire road. Abandoned ties are seen everywhere.

1.2 miles: Straight as an arrow and a small fill is the next feature as the forest continues to surround you.

2.1 miles: Grade crossing of North Road, which has a house or two and some open fields in the area.

3.2 miles: Still in the pine forest with some dairy meadows on the right. Be on the lookout for cows that sometimes stray onto the trail.

3.4 miles: A small wooden bridge that crosses a stream.

3.5 miles: Dairy farm here with a barn that has seen better days.

3.6 miles: Grade crossing of a dirt road that is a driveway for the Tack Shack, an equestrian supply center.

3.8-4.0 miles: A fill begins to build under the trail and a pond appears on the left.

4.1 miles: This is the effective end of the line as the major highway Route 101 is dead ahead. This is a divided highway with no provision for crossing bikes, pedestrians, etc. In the planning stages is a tunnel under the road for trail users. It will be finished in all probability around 1996. It will then connect with other rail-trails at the site of Epping Station.

Storm clouds over the Rockingham Recreational Trail

18 Sugar River Recreational Trail

Endpoints: Belknap Avenue, Newport, New Hampshire, to Route 103 in Claremont, New Hampshire.
Location: Sullivan County, New Hampshire, towns of Newport and Claremont
Length: 10.1 miles
Surface: Gravel and original ballast

Uses:

To get there: Take I 91 to the exit for Claremont, NH and Rte 103. Follow 103 to Newport, then from the center of Newport head North on Rte 10 for 1/4 mile, turn left onto Belknap Ave. Parking Area is 1/10 mile up on the right, next to the Newport Recreation Department

Contact:
Paul Gray, Chief, Department of Trails
New Hampshire Department of Resources and Economic Development
P.O. Box 856
Concord, NH 03302
603-271-3254

Local resources for bike repairs/rentals:
Bob Skinner's Bike Shop, Rte 103, Mt. Sunapee, 603-763-2303.
Claremont Cyclesport, 32 Tremont Sq., Claremont, 603-542-2453.

The Sugar River and this old branch of the Boston and Maine are twins, as they wind down together to the Connecticut River at Claremont, New Hampshire. The line from Concord to Claremont was completed in 1872, and the Boston & Maine, (B&M), ran the line until 1954. The B&M then sold it to shortline entrepreneur Samuel Pinsly. The Pinsly group did an admirable job of running the railroad and servicing the industrial base in Claremont. Dwindling traffic, however, forced them to abandon the track between Newport and West Concord in the early 1960s. The section that we're concerned with today, between East Claremont and Newport, was abandoned in 1977.

There is something special about this trail. The number, type, and frequency of bridges makes it worth the trip. Along this trail there are actually two covered bridges that were designed for rail traffic and are still standing. These structures are a monument to their designers and the state of New Hampshire for their foresight in preserving this heritage.

Before you begin, it may be worthwhile to visit the Newport Station located just off the downtown area in Depot Square. It is in excellent condition, complete with semaphore signal and is in everyday use as a day-care facility.

Interesting shadows inside a truss bridge over the Sugar River.

0.2 miles: Going past the propane dealer we encounter a whistle marker, used at one time to tell the engineer to announce the train's arrival at the crossing.

0.4 miles: Here is the first of many crossings over the Sugar River. This one is a truss bridge built by the American Bridge Co. in 1908. Just over the bridge is a pleasant antique shop with interesting local artifacts.

0.6 miles: Small road crossing with a gate to prevent the entry of cars.

0.8 miles: Passing by a farm with some beautiful meadows.

2.9 miles: Here we pass over a twin bridge. This time a thru truss type, and a deck-girder. Looking below will find some fly fishermen. They've told me that this river has the best game fish in mid-state New Hampshire.

3.0 miles: A small deck-girder bridge is put behind us now as you make your way down stream to Claremont.

3.1 miles: Thru-girder bridge is here and shortly beyond, is the ruins of a small building that probably had some railroad-related purpose.

3.3 miles: Thru-truss bridge is found here along with more scenic beauty.

3.6 miles: A small wooden bridge is encountered here. This allows a steam to pass underneath to get to the main river.

18. Sugar River Recreational Trail

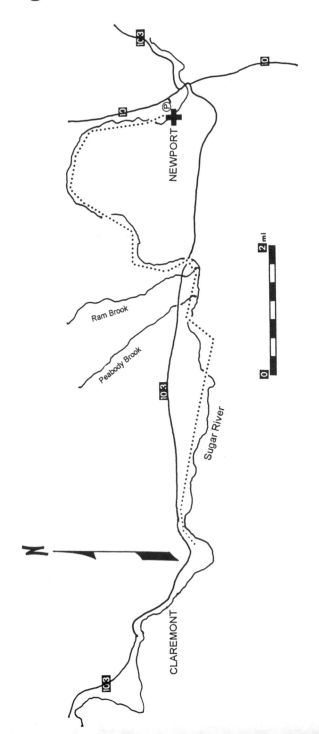

5.2 miles: Highway 11-103 passes overhead on an impressive concrete arch bridge. This bridge is scheduled for some reconstruction work during 1995, so you may find a slight detour around the work site.

5.3 miles: Ram and Peabody Brooks are crossed on small wooden bridges.

6.1 miles: Here is one of the two covered railroad bridges still left on this line. An impressive structure, it is of the Town-Pratt Lattice-Truss type. This is a quiet place to stop and enjoy the surroundings and soft scent of the pine forest.

6.4 miles: Here is a small marker with the inscription "49/27." This marks miles to major division points on the railroad.

6.6 miles: You now cross a well maintained, dirt road and follow parallel to it for about 1/2 mile when it disappears again, into the woods.

7.0 miles: You are now on some original ties. This is the only place where they are found on the trail, they are badly deteriorated and not a nuisance at all.

7.5 miles: Here is another covered bridge of the same type as before. This is the archetypal New England branch-line with its ubiquitous covered bridges and its meandering sense of mission through the woods to the next town.

8.8 miles: Small wooden bridge here.

9.1 miles: Another small wooden bridge here.

10.1 miles: Here we come upon Route 103 again. The original rail is still in place, but no trains will be found. Instead you can continue into town for the usual assortment of fast-food convenience stores and back into the late twentieth century. A small parking lot is being constructed here for the convenience of trail users. This should be finished by mid 1995.

One of the covered railroad bridges on the Sugar River Trail.

19 Wolfeboro/Sanbornville Recreational Trail

Endpoints: Wolfeboro passenger station, off Rte 28, Wolfeboro, New Hampshire, to Roundtable Park at Rte 109, Sanbornville, New Hampshire.
Location: Carroll County New Hampshire. Passing through the towns of Wolfeboro, Brookfield, and Sanbornville, New Hampshire.
Length: 12 miles in two sections
To get there: Wolfeboro is located on the eastern shore of Lake Winnipesaukee. NH Route 28 will lead to the center of Wolfeboro where the old passenger station is found. This is the start of the trail.

Wolfeboro Section

> **Length:** 1 mile
> **Surface:** Crushed stone
>
> **Uses:** 🚶 🚲 ♿ 
>
> **Contact:**
> Town of Wolfeboro
> P.O. Box 629, Wolfeboro, NH 03894
> 603-569-3900

Lake Wentworth State Park Section

> **Length:** 11 miles
> **Surface:** Dirt along side inactive rails
>
> **Uses:** 🚶 🎣 ⛷ 🚤 🚲 🏇 
>
> **Contact:**
> Paul Gray, Chief of Off-Highway Vehicles
> New Hampshire Dept. of Resources and Economic Development
> Trails Bureau
> P.O. Box 856, Concord, NH 03302
> 603-271-3254
>
> Steve LaBonte, President
> Cotton Valley Rail-trail Club
> P.O. Box 155, Mount Vernon, NH 03057-0155
> 603-672-3559

Local resources for bike repair/rentals:
Nordic Skier, Main Street, Wolfeboro, 603-569-3151

Gingerbread Victorian Wolfeboro Passenger Station.

The resort community of Wolfeboro, New Hampshire, had rail service starting in August, 1872, via the Eastern Railroad. By the early years of this century there were seven passenger stations on the 12-mile branch from Sanbornville. These were at Sanbornville, Brookfield, Fernald, Lake Wentworth, Wolfeboro Falls, Wolfeboro, and Lake Station. This last one was close to the main station in downtown Wolfeboro, but right on the lake to meet the railroad-owned steam ships that were a popular way to get to the other resort communities of Lake Winnipesaukee. The building is still there and is used as a restaurant.

The Boston & Maine Railroad acquired the branch in 1892, when it was taking over all Eastern Railroad assets. The boom years were then underway, and extensive engine servicing facilities were built at the Sanbornville junction with the B & M mainline. It was named a division headquarters, which meant that the clerk functions were performed here, in addition to the maintenance of the locomotives. This made Sanbornville a busy place indeed, at least until the engine house burned down in 1911. The B&M decided to move the division headquarters to Dover at that time, and the facilities that were then rebuilt in Sanbornville reflected its declining role. In 1922 the B&M sold off the steam ship to a private interest. In 1936 passenger service was discontinued. Freight service continued on a daily basis until the 1950s when it was reduced to tri-weekly service. In the 1960s it was reduced to an as-needed basis.

Fernald Station with ex-Central Vermont, Fairmont motor-car on display.

In 1972 a group of investors led by Donald Hallock bought the branch from the B&M and formed the New Wolfeboro Railroad Company. Mr. Hallock came by way of the Strasburg Railroad in Pennsylvania, a pioneering entity in the tourist railroad industry. He undertook to restore the condition of the structures and track, and bought equipment necessary to run a passenger excursion operation to Sanbornville from Wolfeboro. He also undertook a marketing effort to restore freight service, as he knew that, in order to be successful, the New Wolfeboro Railroad would have to be a dual purpose road.

The tourist operation had a steam engine to pull the old-time passenger cars and met with reasonable prosperity, but the freight situation never took off. The last freight customer was an excelsior mill in Wolfeboro Falls that shipped only an occasional box car of finished product. The operation was abandoned in 1986 and the title to the track and right-of-way was given to the State of New Hampshire's Department of Transportation. Later that year an agreement was reached between the DOT and the Department of Resources and Economic Development, Division of Parks and Recreation, Trails Bureau, to operate the corridor as a recreational trail with the tracks remaining in place. In 1991 the Town of Wolfeboro received permission to construct a multi-use path on the 1/2-mile section within their jurisdiction.

This trail is actually two-in-one. The first is a short but scenic run that passes by the beautifully restored Wolfeboro passenger station, a section of Lake Winnipesaukee, and the ruins of the last on-line customer of the Wolfeboro Railroad. The second part is an 11-mile run that has the tracks still in place. It is possible to single-track-ride or hike along the tracks, though it will be bumpy in some areas as the room is limited.

The Trails-Rails-Action-Committee (TRAC) is the local volunteer group which oversees the interest of the three communities that are part of the trail, Wolfeboro, Wakefield, and Sanbornville. This organization, working under the direction of the state, stays primarily focused on conventional multi-use path functions. Another organization called the Cotton Valley Rail-Trail Club (CVRTC) uses the tracks to run their speeders, putt-putts, and motor cars. CVRTC is a collection of railway motor car enthusiasts and railway historians who have joined together as goodwill ambassadors to promote their hobby and to keep alive the skills and experiences of the rail workers who once kept the nation connected. The club began in the summer of 1992 when a group of New England rail car owners joined with a group of local railroad enthusiasts in Wolfeboro. Together they received permission from the State of New Hampshire to operate rail cars and to maintain a portion of the former Wolfeboro Railroad, including the structures. CVRTC voluntarily maintains 8 miles of rail owned by the state, at no cost to the taxpayers.

Most visible of the Club's achievements was the replacement of broken glass and the repainting of the former Fernald Station on Rt. 109 in Wolfeboro, NH. This building is the club's meeting place. Current projects on the line include filling washouts, replacing ties near the station, and enacting an "adopt-a-mile" program. The CVRTC holds monthly meetings on the second Saturday of each month from March thru November at the Fernald Station on Rt. 109 in Wolfeboro, NH. In addition to the activities in Wolfeboro, the Cotton Valley Rail-Trail Club organizes the following events:

Fun Runs: Family Motor Car events where little or no work is scheduled. The motor cars operate on scenic rail lines, in cooperation with several New England Railroads. A fee is sometimes required. *Work/Rides:* Participants perform a partial day of work for the host railroad, followed by a motor car ride on designated track. *Work Parties:* Host railroad helps provide meals and/or accommodations to workers. Workers use motor cars for transportation to work site(s). (Hard work, but generates goodwill.) The construction season of 1995 will see a team effort of the CVRTC and TRAC to improve the southern causeway and make it a more readily walkable surface.

19. Wolfeboro/Sanbornville Recreational Trail

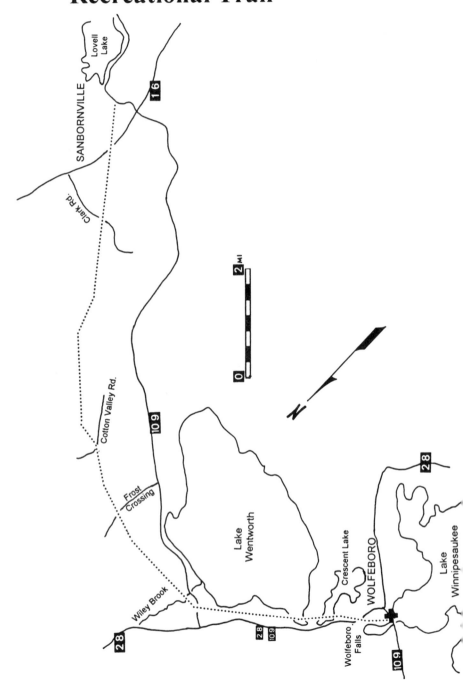

0.0 miles: A perfect place to start. The beautifully restored Wolfeboro passenger station no longer serves trains, but instead serves as the office for the local Chamber of Commerce. Diagonally opposite the passenger station is the freight station, and behind it toward the bay is where a turntable and three-stall roundhouse were once situated.

0.6 miles: Wolfeboro Falls is found here as you cross a bridge with the falls on the right. Park benches and photogenic views are here, along with the remains of the excelsior mill that burned down in 1993. (Excelsior is the term for wood shavings which were used as a packaging material until the success of plastic peanuts made it a forgotten word.) It is in this area that the improved surface ends and the rails are seen again on the other side of the grade crossing of Routes 28 & 109.

0.9 miles: Mast Landing Street grade crossing.

1.2 miles: Whitten Neck is seen here as you traverse Crescent Lake on a 1200-foot causeway.

1.4 miles: Lake Wentworth is crossed here via a causeway like the one previous, but this one is 1800 feet long and it was built with 60,000 tons of granite rip-rap used as the base.

3.1 miles: Fernald Station and the grade crossing of Rt. 109. Fernald is the area where the CVRTC activities can be viewed along with the old B&M engine house and yard area.

Taking advantage of benches on the finished portion of the Wolfeboro Trail.

3.3 miles: Wiley Brook is crossed via a small bridge.

5.1 miles: Grade crossing here is locally known as Frost's Crossing.

6.1 miles: Grade crossing here is Cotton Valley Road. This was the site of the now long-gone passenger station of the same name.

9.9 miles: Brookfield Station was once here as you cross over Clark Road.

11.0 miles: You are now in Wakefield/Sanbornville at the Grade crossing for Route 16. This is a busy highway, so be careful crossing. New Hampshire Northcoast Railroad is off to the left and getting closer to you as approach the final mile.

12.0 miles: You've reached Sanbornville and Turntable Park, a memorial to the town's important railroad heritage. The mainline of the active track is adjacent to you here. If you look to the south across Rt. 109, you'll see a few remaining railroad-constructed buildings.

Roundtable Park in Sanbornville New Hampshire.

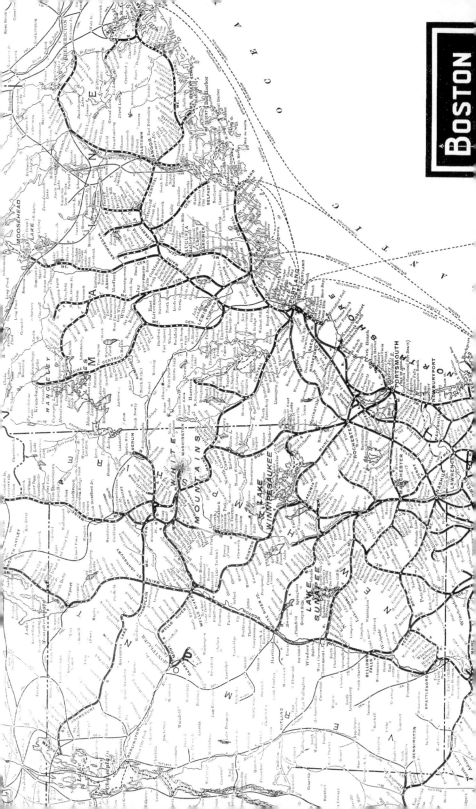

White Mountain National Forest of New Hampshire
Ex-Logging Railroads Converted to Rail-Trails

No book on the outdoors of the Northeast would be complete without a mention of the Appalachian Mountain Club (AMC). It was formed in 1876 and is the oldest recreation and conservation organization in the United States. Today the hut system in the White Mountains of New Hampshire provides accommodations for over 50,000 persons a year. At the club's headquarters in Boston on Joy Street, there is available to members and the general public alike a wealth of information on hiking, camping, and trails. Regularly scheduled meetings and lectures are among the other activities offered. The AMC and the ex-logging railroads of New Hampshire have an interesting symbiotic relationship.

In the 1870s, as the public came to the resorts of the White Mountains via the railroads, they became more familiar with the way the logging operations were being handled. Clear cuts of entire mountains, with piles of debris known as slash (end pieces, branches, and other waste) opened the way for enormous forest fires. The people who patronized the resorts were appalled at this devastation. These patrons were not the working class types, but the elite from the large cities of Boston and New York. An outcry ensued that was heard in Washington, D.C. The Weeks Act of 1911 caused the creation of the White Mountain National Forest, a direct result of the protest against the rape of this area by the numerous logging companies.

None of the loggers responsible for the destruction were as efficient at this trade as the J.E. Henry & Sons Company. They perfected the practice of clear-cutting, using a railroad for getting out the timber and stomping out opposition by intimidation or arrogance. Some of the largest forest fires in the eastern United States were on land owned by the Henry Company. The mark of these fires can still be seen today in some of the more remote areas of the White Mountains (when viewed from the air).

Gradually the vast reserves of marketable timber were depleted and the narrow gauge railroads that carried the logs out were dismantled. These then formed the nucleus of the network of trails now existing in the National Forest. Some are listed as being "part of a railroad." This usually means that these railroads had a switch-back that was not part of the hiking trail. The switch-back was used to ease the grade for the locomotive, not so important for hikers who gravitated to steeper terrain.

An excellent book on this subject is *Logging Railroads of the White Mountains,* by C. Francis Belcher. This was published by the AMC in 1980 and is still available today. It is the last word on the subject.

View of the White Mountains, Pemigewasset District -- photo by Bruce Scofield

The majority of these ex-logging railroad trails are managed by the United States Forest Service and are organized by district. Maps of these areas are available from the various trail managers or the Appalachian Mountain Club. The following is a list of trails that can be traveled by foot, mountain bike, cross-country skis, horse, snowmobile, or ATV. For more information, consult the district rangers or the book *500 Great Rail-Trails: A Directory of Multi-Use Paths Created from Abandoned Railroads,* produced by the Rails-to-Trails Conservancy (Living Planet Press, 1993).

A. Pemigewasset Ranger District
B. Saco Ranger District
C. Evans Notch Ranger District
D. Ammonoosuc Ranger District
E. Androscoggin Ranger District

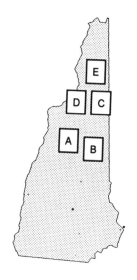

Pemigewasset Ranger District

Contact:
Jim DiMaio, District Ranger
RFD 3, Box 15, Plymouth, NH 03264
1-603-536-1310

Cedar Brook Trail
Ethan Pond Trail
Franconia Brook Trail
Lincoln Woods Trail
Thoreau Falls Trail
Wilderness Trail

Saco Ranger District

Contact:
Robert Walker, District Ranger
Kancamagus Highway, RFD 1, Box 94
Conway, NH 03818
1-603-447-5448

Dry River Trail
East Branch Trail
Flat Mountain Pond Trail
Guinea Pond Trail
Oliverian Trail
Rob Brook Trail
Rocky Branch Trail
Sawyer River Trail
Upper Nanamocomuck Trail

Evans Notch Ranger District

Contact:
Rollie Ortegon, District Ranger
RR2, Box 2270, Bethel, ME 04217
1-207-824-2134

Moriah Brook Trail
Shelburne Trail
Wild River Trail

Ammonoosuc Ranger District

Contact:
Paul Shaw, District Ranger
P.O. Box 239, Bethlehem, NH 03574
1-603-869-2626

North Twin Trail
Zealand Trail

Androscoggin Ranger District

Contact:
Katherine Bulchis, District Ranger
80 Glen Road, Gorham, NH 03581-1399
1-603-466-2713

West Milan Trail
York Pond Trail

View of the White Mountains -- photo by Bruce Scofield

THE NEW YORK,
NEW HAVEN AND HARTFORD RAILROAD CO.
OPERATED AND CONTROLLED LINES

Great Rail-Trails of Rhode Island

20. East Bay Bicycle Path
21. Trestle Trail

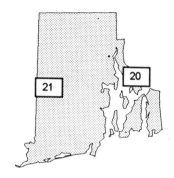

The two Rhode Island rail-trails represent different ends of a spectrum, in terms of completion as well as geography. The East Bay Trail is paved, located in a bustling urban area near the ocean, and is used by thousands each month. The Trestle Trail, on the other hand, travels through lonely woods, marshes, and areas where you'll probably see more beavers than people. On the Trestle Trail you should expect some sandy and wet surfaces, some washboard surfaces, and a challenging bridge. Do not let these conditions prevent you from trying it out, however, as there are lovely and quaint small villages found along the way. Many of the trails in this book pass through towns that are reminiscent of times past, but the two villages on the Trestle Trail (Greene and Summit) are special in that they owe their existence quite literally to the railroad. They will not be forgotten places much longer because the East Coast Greenway (Boston to Washington DC) will be passing by.

Try to take time to visit the Trestle Trail, take its rural beauty and its unusual little villages. This trail's qualities are in part due to the efforts of Ginny Leslie, Senior Planner for the State of Rhode Island's Department of Environmental Management. Of all the people contacted in the research of this book, none was more helpful or ready to assist with old maps and other materials. She is almost a one-woman Chamber of Commerce for the Coventry area, as well as being a history buff.

The East Bay Trail is another gem. You'll be on the shore of Narragansett Bay for miles, savoring the salt air the whole time. The beauty here is so astounding that you'll forget that this line was mostly known for innovative technology. This was the first non-traction railroad in the country to be electrified.

Enjoy the Rail-Trails of Rhode Island.

20 East Bay Bicycle Path

End Points: Independence Park, Bristol, Rhode Island, to India Point Park, Providence, Rhode Island. Passing through the towns of Barrington and Warren along the way.

Location: Bristol County Rhode Island. Greater Providence, Barrington, Warren and Bristol are the towns passed through.

Length: 14.5 miles

Surface: Asphalt

Uses:

To get there: The best place to start this trail is in Bristol at Independence Park. This is reached by following Route 114 out of Providence to Bristol.

Contact:
Kevin O'Malley, Regional Manager
Colt State Park
Bristol, RI 02809
401-253-7482

Local resources for bike repairs/rentals:
Bay Path Cycles Inc., 13 State Street, Bristol, RI., 401-254-1277
Your Bike Shop, 51 Cole Street, Warren, RI., 401-245-9755

Bridge over the Palmer River

Watchemoket Cove and the Providence sky-line in the distance.

The East Bay Bike Path gets its name from its location on the east side of Narragansett Bay. It follows the right-of -way of the old New Haven Railroad. This is one of the best bike paths in New England.

The original railroad was known as the Providence, Warren, and Bristol Railroad. Formed in the mid-19th century boom years of railroad construction, it served primarily as a passenger line from the capitol of Providence to the suburb of Bristol. A branch that diverged off at Warren provided service to Fall River, Massachusetts. When these lines were absorbed by the New Haven Railroad in 1893 as part of a package deal to complete the "Shoreline" route, they became the nucleus of an experiment to try a new technology .... electrification. This was the first time in the United States that electricity was used to power an all-season main-line. The venture flourished and was so successful that the line between Providence and Warren was up-graded and double tracked.

In the early years of this century this line also was part of a freight operation to Newport via a ferry at Bristol. Normally the end of the line was at Bristol, but there was plenty of business along the way. The well-protected and deep harbor at East Providence was good for ocean vessel cargo transfers. Several large oil companies such as Mobil, Gulf, and Amoco maintained facilities right up to the end of rail service. Warren had two textile mills that were big customers and Bristol had a rubber company along Hereshoff's Shipyard, builder of America's Cup Yachts. There was also the usual mix of customers that could be found on any railroad.

Overcast day on the East Bay Trail

With the onset of the private automobile, the aging of railroad equipment, and the general slowdown caused by the Great Depression, the management of the New Haven Railroad was forced to re-examine the situation and "pull the plug" on the electric service and convert the line to conventional steam power in 1932.

The Hurricane of 1938 brought extensive damage, which resulted in the line becoming single-tracked and freight only, though there was an occasional week-end excursion that brought out the passengers in the summer months. Freight service continued, but in the fifties it was reduced to a tri-weekly run to Bristol.

In 1968 the Penn-Central was formed and the New Haven Railroad disappeared into it. Many obscure NH branch lines were abandoned at this time, and the Bristol branch was among them. Officially abandoned in 1973, the rails soon after were pulled out and sold to the scrapper. Eventually the right-of-way was up-graded and turned over to the Rhode Island Department of Environmental Management in four stages starting in 1986. The trail was completed in 1994.

You'll notice right away the quality paving job and superior markings on the pavement denoting boundaries and hazards. A first class trail is here. This trip will be a memorable one, so be sure to take your camera!

0.0 miles: We're starting at beautiful Independence Park. Overlooking the Bay, it provides a good place to have a picnic, launch a boat, or start a bike ride. Nearby restaurants, some of which are open 24 hours, provide necessary food stuffs. The trail curves around the harbor, and there are some architecturally pleasing condos located nearby with stunning perennial gardens.

0.4 miles: Poppasquash Road grade crossing.

0.5 miles: A salt water marsh, and then a pond that seems to have a direct connection to the harbor. Look for the Loons, other aquatic birds, and another stunning display of perennials located along the trail.

1.1 miles: Grade crossing at Asylum Road. Del's mobile kiosk is one of many places to have a cold soda. Look here for the quince bushes nearby and the unusual ivy planted. Big rip-rap is used in this area also to stabilize the bank.

1.4 miles: Grade crossing at Fales Road.

1.5 miles: Split-rail fence helps provide a boundary to the nearby houses, some of which have unusual rock gardens. Slight up-grade to the next grade crossing.

1.6 miles: Mulberry Road grade crossing.

1.8 miles: Gibson Road grade crossing. Ocean is seen just on the left.

2.0 miles: This grade crossing is Aaron Avenue.

2.1 miles: Peck Rock Road grade crossing and an expansive hedgerow.

2.8 miles: North Farm Road grade crossing.

2.9 miles: The boundary with Warren, Rhode Island.

3.3 miles: Going past Locust trees at the intersection with Locust Terrace.

3.4 miles: Grade crossing at Bradford Street.

3.6 miles: Grade crossing at Beach Street.

3.7 miles: The Lester M. Derissio Bike Path Tunnel. Made of precast concrete, it carries a street over the rail-trail.

3.9 miles: Grade crossing at Haile Street, followed by Route 114 and Burr Hills Park. You're in a busy urban area, so use caution when crossing the roads.

3.9 miles: Grade Crossing of Cherry Street.

4.0 miles: Grade Crossing of Franklin Street. This area was the junction for the branch to Fall River. Situated just south of here, the line curved away to the southeast, but is long gone now.

4.3 miles: Here is an interesting old building that apparently has a railroad past. It currently houses a natural foods cafe and a sports medicine office. The municipal parking area across from here has recycled railroad ties as a divider from the trail. This area was also the southern end of the double track and the site of the Warren Station.

4.4 miles: Grade crossing of Child Street. Del's Deli and Paul's Deli cater to the trail's users, so you will meet fellow travelers here.

4.5 miles: Slight down-grade here as you go past the crossing of Wood Street.

4.6 miles: Hope Street and a power sub-station. This site was used by the electric company for many years, and at one time, had a generating plant to power the overhead wires for the trains. Norbert Street is also in this area, as well as an antique whistle marker made of concrete and of an unusual shape.

20. East Bay Bicycle Path

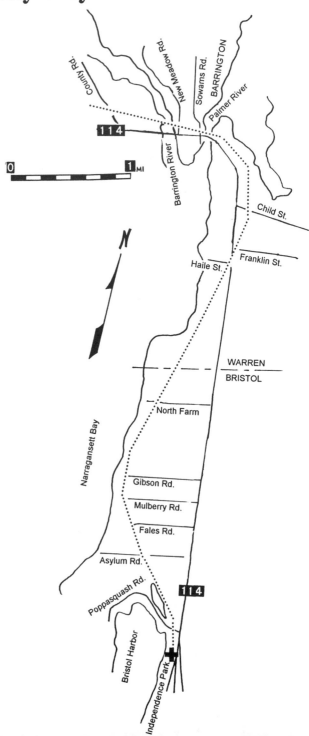

4.9 miles: Kelly Street is crossed now. Here at one time on your right was the North Warren Station. American Tourister's main manufacturing complex is coming upon us now. This mill was a good customer of the New Haven Railroad. Trucks provide all the transportation today, but the dormant and rusted rails can be seen within the complex.

5.1 miles: Crossing over the Palmer River via a wooden trestle. This is a most impressive span, long and photogenic from the parallel-running Route 114. The Town of Barrington lies on the other side of the bridge.

5.2 miles: Crossing at Sowams Road.

5.4 miles: Crossing at New Meadow Road. Shortly after is another big wooden trestle over a salt water inlet called the Barrington River.

5.9 miles: Busy grade crossing of County Road. Be careful here, as it is heavily traveled and there are many commercial businesses in the area.

6.2 miles: The trail has an outlet here for the Gourmet Pantry.

6.4 miles: Crossing West Street. With a baseball field here, this spot looks like small-town America.

6.7 miles: A medical office building is located here, and Brickyard Pond can be seen on the left with its abundance of bird life. The personnel within the complex are probably encouraged to walk this beautiful trail during their lunch hour. This area is just one example of pride that a rail-trail can instill in the neighbors. Just look at the beautiful plantings seen around this area that are meant for the pleasure of trail travelers.

7.3 miles: Middle Highway grade crossing. In the summer months you can find an entrepreneur selling frozen ice coolers at a kiosk nearby.

7.4 miles: Grade crossing at South Lake Drive.

8.1 miles: Grade crossing at Washington Road.

8.3 miles: Grade crossing of Alfred Drowne Road.

8.5 miles: Crossing of Bay Spring Avenue. Here also can be found an old industrial complex that at one time used a water tower.

9.0 miles: Narragansett Avenue will be crossed here. Haines State Park is nearby with picnic tables and facilities. On your left is scenic Bullock Cove with an anchorage for boats.

9.1 miles: Vintner Avenue is bisected at the border into East Providence.

9.3 miles: Grade crossing of busy Crescent View Avenue Be careful here.

9.5 miles: You can rest here and watch what's happening at a salt pond and tidal flat area. The Bullock Cove Bridge has been recently re-done and is worth a look. If you happen along at the right time, the tidal surge is impressive.

9.8 miles: Outlet to Herman Street.

10.3 miles: Intersection with Turner Avenue and the urban area known as Riverside Square. Here also is the old New Haven passenger station still serving the public, but now known as Callegaro's Deli. It is a fine place to sip a soda or get a sub. There are other casual restaurants and ice cream shops nearby that cater to the trail clientele, as well as bike shops aimed at getting bikes repaired and back out onto the trail as quickly as possible.

20 East Bay Bicycle Path

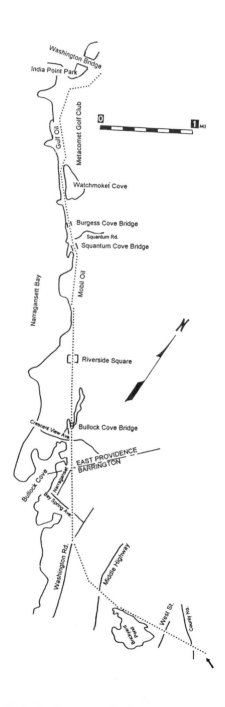

10.5 miles: Grade crossing of Washington Street; then passing under Rte 114.
10.8 miles: A good view of Narragansett Bay is seen from here, with small fleets of sailboats mixed in with ocean vessel traffic.
11.0 miles: Passing the Narragansett Bay Lighthouse on the approach to Providence. Going down-grade. There are extensive petroleum off-loading facilities nearby and an overhead oil pipeline goes across the trail.
11.1 miles: Grade crossing of Mobil Road, named for the oil company. Also in this area is an intact rail siding used at one time for the transfer of oils and lubricants to many points in New England.
11.7 miles: Still going by oil facilities and then over the Squantum Cove Bridge.
12.0 miles: Grade crossing at Squantum Road. In the days of passenger service this area had its own stop, listed on the timetable as "Squantum."The large mansion on the left is known as the Squantum Association, an exclusive club that has, for many years, been an integral part of the Providence social scene.
12.4 miles: Crossing over the Burgess Cove Bridge and the grade crossing over Amoco Road.
12.6 miles: Here can be seen a remnant of the rail days. On the right as you head south is a metal post assembly that was once used to place long pieces of rail. These "racks" were used by the track gangs to store the rail at areas that were known to have frequent problems.
12.7 miles: A tidal pond known as Watchemoket Cove, which has a bridge over its connection to the ocean. Swans are frequent visitors.
12.8 miles: The trail now moves sharply East and uphill to avoid going through the Gulf Oil facility which is now closed. As you crest the hill you are on the sidewalk at Veteran's Memorial Parkway, a busy street, so be careful.
13.2 miles: You are now going by the East Providence Gulf Oil Terminal's main entrance, and across the street is the Metacomet Golf Club.
13.5 miles: Veteran's Memorial Parkway overlook and parking area.
14.0 miles: Ramp to Washington Bridge to Providence.
14.5 miles: The end of path is behind the Days Inn Hotel and across the street from the India Point Park in Providence.

21 Trestle Trail

Endpoints: Hill Farm Road, Coventry Center, Rhode Island and ending at the Connecticut border town of Oneco, at the grade crossing with Route 14A.
Location: Kent County, Rhode Island, passing through the towns of Coventry, Summit, Greene, and ending at Oneco, Connecticut.
Length: 7.7 miles
Surface: Original ballast and gravel.

Uses:

To get there: Take Rte 117 into Coventry and then go south on Hill Farm Road, near Coventry Center. Just before the Coventry Men's Club, take a right into a small dirt parking lot. This is the starting point for the east end, and the trail begins just beyond the concrete blocks which prevent automobile access. The Oneco end is located on Rt. 14A, 1/2 mile west of the junction with Rt. 14.
Contact:
Ginny Leslie, Senior Planner
Rhode Island Department of Environmental Management
Division of Planning and Development
83 Park Street, Providence, RI 02903
401-277-2776 ext 4309
Local resources for bike repairs/rentals:
Greenway Cycles, 579 Washington Street, Coventry, 401-822-2080.

Coventry, Rhode Island's famous son was Nathaniel Greene, a general in the Revolutionary War. When the Hartford, Providence, and Fishkill Railroad completed construction in this area in 1854, they named a small town that was being developed on the line in his honor. "Greene" became a thriving cultural and commercial center. In 1898 the New Haven Railroad took over all the assets of the New York and New England Railroad, the successor road to the old Fishkill. This section became part of the New Haven's Midland Division. As soon as the New Haven took over this line, it experienced a decline in traffic due to the more favorable routing of the Shoreline Division.

The New Haven abandoned the 18 miles between Coventry, Rhode Island, and Plainfield, Connecticut, in 1967. The successor road Penn-Central then sold the right-of-way to Narragansett Electric Company to use as a power transmission line, but it was never built. Narragansett Electric then donated the land to the State of Rhode Island in 1992.

The Providence and Worcester Railroad was a modern regional railroad re-incarnation of the old New Haven, and was the last to operate several old sections of the old Hartford, Providence, and Fishkill Railroad (HP&F). Those sections ran from Willimantic to Plainfield by way of South Windham and Versailles. That line is now out of service between Willimantic and Versailles, but the Eastern Connecticut Chapter of the National Railroad Historical Society hopes to institute a tourist train on the section near Willimantic.

Another section of the HP&F was most recently known as the Washington Secondary, which ran from Providence to Coventry, is out of service also. The Rhode Island Department of Transportation is negotiating to purchase this portion of the line in West Warwick and Cranston. The Town of Coventry owns the right-of-way in eastern Coventry, the entire 24-mile line from Connecticut to the Amtrak (ex-New Haven Shoreline Division) in Cranston, which will soon be in public ownership.

The Trestle Trail is one of two trails to sample in Rhode Island, and it is a diamond in the rough. Some areas have a washboard surface and there are a few water hazards to negotiate, one being a missing deck on a 35-foot bridge over a fairly deep stream, but it is crossable without much effort. The other area is under Rt. 102 where a spring seems be providing an unending supply of water. Not too much has been done to up-grade the physical characteristics of the trail yet, but there are plans in the works. The East Coast Greenway (Boston to Washington DC) will pass through Rhode Island by way of the Trestle Trail.

Monument to the Railroad at Greene, RI.

21. Trestle Trail

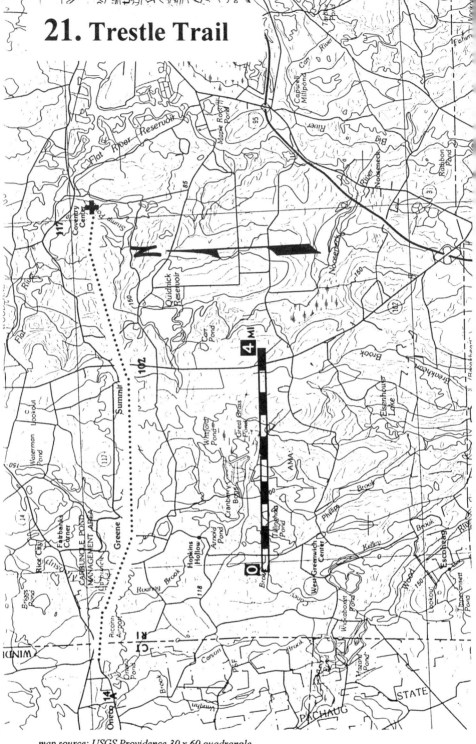

map source: USGS Providence 30 x 60 quadrangle

0.1 miles: Deck-girder bridge crosses the northeast corner of the Coventry Reservoir, sometimes called Stump Pond. The deck of this bridge is now surfaced with aircraft landing mats.

0.4 miles: Reservoir is still on the left as a big fill develops here.

0.7 miles: Signs of some old rotting ties as the fill turns into a moss-lined cut.

1.5 miles: A cut is found here and then it opens up to a wider trail.

1.6 miles: In this area you'll find a bridge missing, but the small stream is easily forded. Big cut granite blocks are the only remnants of the original bridge.

2.0 miles: Sandy surface here is from a washout of a paved road that comes close to the trail.

2.2 miles: On a fill here that is partially washed out.

2.6 miles: Sharply uphill to West Hill Road, and then down sharply to the trail again. A bridge must have been here at one time.

3.3 miles: Route 102 will pass overhead and it may be wet in this area. The best way through is to the right on a narrow shoulder.

3.7 miles: Small feed and grain store here appears to have been at one time rail-served. A horse farm and a smattering of houses form part of a village called Summit. Formerly known as Perry's Hollow, it was re-named after the railroad came through in 1856, because it was the highest point on the line. Buildings of interest here include the Summit Baptist Church (1865) and the Summit Free Library (1885). Both are on Rte 117, Flat River Road.

3.9 miles: On a filled-in section as a marsh encloses the trail. This area has seen a rise in the water level due to the work of some beavers.

4.2 miles: A beautifully dense and fragrant pine forest.

5.0 miles: You've reached the 35-foot bridge with the missing deck. The stream it crosses is about 18"-to-36"deep. The girders themselves are about 18" across and do not present a difficult challenge. It's your choice, either a little wet or a little brave. The approaches to the bridge sit on an ascending fill until it reaches approximately 20 feet above the surrounding marsh land.

5.1 miles: Outlet here to a residential neighborhood and side street that runs parallel to the trail for a short distance in the village of Greene. In the late 19th century, Greene was an important stop on the milk train that ran to Providence, as much of the city's dairy goods came the farms here.

5.2 miles: A lonely telegraph pole is seen here with one cross-arm and no insulators intact.

5.3 miles: Here stands a set of railroad car wheels on a pedestal, with an inscription on a plaque that serves to commemorate the 125th anniversary of the coming of the railroad. A grade crossing of Railroad Avenue is also here.

5.6 miles: You pass into a pine forest again and experience a feeling of claustrophobia as the greenery encroaches and you are heading up a slight grade. An interesting series of low stone retaining walls is seen here also.

Bridge over Coventry Reservoir with young fishermen on it.

6.1 miles: Grade crossing at Lewis Farm Road. North-South Trail (light blue blazes) goes onto the Trestle Trail. This is a trail in the making and will eventually run about 75 miles from the Massachusetts border to the southern coast.

6.4 miles: The trail's namesake bridge, the *Trestle* over the Moosup River. This is a "finished for trail use" bridge. It is an older restoration, has chain link fence sides, and shows some signs of neglect. But it is a safe and pleasant alternative to the previous bridges encountered thus far. The Moosup River meanders across the low marsh areas under the bridge about 50 feet below you.

6.5-6.6 miles: The North-South Trail exits here to the right.

6.7 miles: Just as the trail starts to bend to the left, you'll notice a path down to the right. This leads to Carbuncle Pond Fishing Access Area, located on Rt. 14 just east of the border with Connecticut.

7.3 miles: The border of Connecticut.

7.7 miles: As you enter a residential neighborhood in Oneco, Connecticut, you'll cross over Rte 14A and reach the end of this trail.

Bicyclists enjoying the trail

Great Rail-Trails of Vermont

The Great Rail-Trails of Vermont are widely distributed throughout the state. Vermont has a good variety of Rail-Trails that are fun, historic, memorable, and are, on the whole, the best maintained in the northeast. The rural ones are part of the vast network of snowmobile trails that criss-cross the state. The Alburg area of Lake Champlain was once home to some of New England's greatest water crossings by a railroad. Most of the buildings that were rail-related are gone but the beauty of the region is now the focus of the trip.

The Burlington Waterfront Bikeway is located within the largest city in Vermont and is a wonderful trail. Similar to the East Bay Trail in Rhode Island in terms of planning and finish, it has been well received by the locals and the pride they take in their trail is evident. The Central Vermont Trail passes through some of this state's best dairy land, and it is a pleasant journey that should not be missed. The small city of St. Albans, with its interesting history, is an enjoyable side trip along the CV Trail.

The D&H Trail goes through some of the most spectacular scenery in New England. The small towns of Castleton and Poultney are off the beaten path and are unspoiled by the tourist invasion that has changed other parts of Vermont. In the New York parts of this trail, the politics of Rail-Trails reached a boiling point. Consequently, it is necessary to recommend that you do not cross into New York on this trail yet. Perhaps in the near future that will change. The Montpelier & Wells River Trail is a rural trail that is well maintained and very wooded. Though abandoned about 40 years ago, it still has a railroad feel to it and is definitely worth a trip. Beautiful forest lakes and mountains nearby make for a scenic tour.

MAP OF THE

CENTRAL VERMONT

RAILROAD

And its Connections.

22 Alburg Rail-Trail

Endpoints: Alburg Industrial Park, Alburg, Vermont, to 100 yards west of the Central Vermont Railway Trestle over Lake Champlain at East Alburg, Vermont.
Location: Grand Isle County, Alburg, to, East Alburg, Vermont.
Length: 3.5 miles
Surface: Cinder and Gravel

Uses:

To get there: Take I-89 north to Exit 21 in Swanton VT. Then follow Route 78 West to Route 2 North into Alburg. As you get into town you can park anywhere that is clearly marked as approved or safe. The trail starts across the street from the Volunteer Fire Station at the rear of the Industrial Park.
Contact:
Trails Coordinator, Department of Parks and Recreation
111 West Street, Essex Junction, VT 05452
802-879-6565

Mr. Philip R. Pearo, President.
Alburg Sno-Springers Snowmobile Club.
Box 122, Alburg, VT 05440
802-796-3341
Local resources for bike repairs/rentals:
Earl's Cycling & Fitness, 135 Main St., Burlington, 802-862-4203

This trail is in northern Vermont and holds a special place in the history of New England railroads. It was a branch of the Central Vermont Railway and it was used for two purposes: (1) To interchange with the Rutland Railroad at Alburg, Vermont; and (2) to cross over Lake Champlain and interchange with the Delaware and Hudson Railroad at Rousses Point, New York.

The Rutland Railroad arrived at Alburg the hard way, across the water. Heading north out of Burlington, the line crossed onto South Hero Island via a three-mile-long causeway made of giant marble blocks from some of Vermont's famous stone quarries. Continuing north, it entered North Hero Island via another causeway by crossing the Gut, a body of water at Bow Arrow Point. The line traversed water once more as it crossed onto the Alburg Tongue's southernmost area at Pelot's Point. It finally arrived at the north end of the peninsula at Alburg and joined with the Central Vermont. Together they headed west across more water to Rousses Point, New York. These long causeways carrying the rails were the talk of engineering circles for many years in the early part of this century.

There were only two other railroad causeways in the United States that were better known than this series in Vermont. The Florida East Coast Railroad's line to Key West, destroyed in a 1930s hurricane, was the best known. This line connected all the islands to the mainland of South Florida, and carried the crack passenger trains of the era to Key West, the tourist mecca. The other famous crossing was the Southern Pacific Railroad's great Lucin cutoff across the Great Salt Lake in Utah. Neither of these railroads had to endure the bitter New England winters that plagued this Vermont line for the sixty years it ran the length of Lake Champlain.

Montreal-bound passenger trains once ran through here every day. Famous "name trains" such as the daytime *Green Mountain Flyer* and the nighttime *Mt. Royal* were among them. The main traffic, however, was derived from the milk trains which stopped at nearly every dairy farm and other small depots strategically located along the way. Each farmer would transfer to the railroad his 100-quart cans of milk in small or large groups, depending on his farm's size. The multiple stops required of each train gave rise to the term "milk run."

When the Rutland was abandoned in 1963, the causeways leading to the south to Burlington were dismantled, but signs of their existence can still be found today, if you look hard enough. Most of the marble blocks are still there. The timber causeway west of Alburg and leading to Rousses Point was a joint Central Vermont and Rutland-owned structure. The CV was not interested in maintaining it alone, so it was dismantled when they abandoned the branch from their East Alburg causeway.

This relatively small section of the Lake Champlain crossings is today's only remaining segment, and is crossed daily by CN-NECR freights in each direction. A swing-type draw bridge is here and manned as necessary boat traffic dictates. Amtrak's *Montrealer* used to come through here until it was discontinued due to budget constraints. The new Amtrak train, *The Vermonter*, subsidized by the State of Vermont, goes only as far as Burlington.

175

22. Alburg Rail-Trail

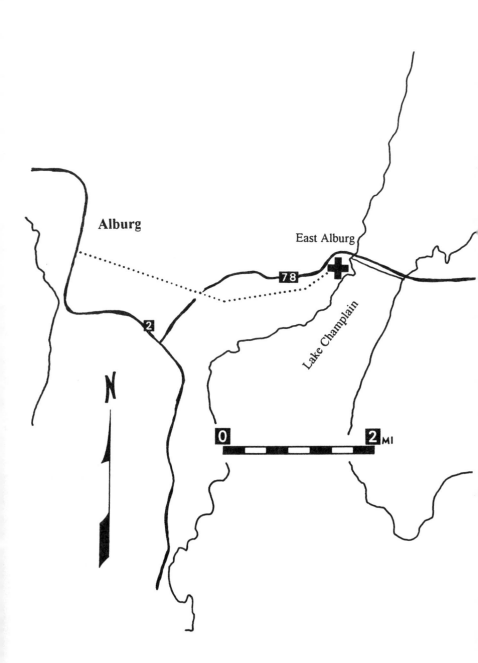

0.0 miles: Start of the trail is at the rear of the Industrial Park, in the center of town. Notice the coal used as a mulch in the traffic circle in the Industrial Park. This area was once the interchange yard between the Rouses Point branch of the Central Vermont Railway and the Rutland Railroad. Both roads continued west across Route 2 and crossed Lake Champlain, a few miles beyond, via a rickety, mile-long timber causeway. This is long gone, but the timber piers can still be seen. As you get onto the trail, you'll notice that it is fairly well-kept and comfortable to ride.

0.4 miles: Here you'll come upon a bit of a swamp or marsh on your left and a farm on the right. In certain areas on this trail you'll notice there is a parallel-running roadbed on your right. This was the original alignment of the road bed.

0.6 miles: The wetlands patch on the left is becoming a more open and bird-filled tract. It is a state-owned wildlife refuge known as the Mud Creek Waterfowl Area, known the world over for its variety of waterfowl. Come here in the late summer and you can see great masses of geese and ducks heading south or a Great Blue Heron doing his ungainly dance across the mud-flats.

1.6 miles: The trail is basically cinder and coal with patches of grass, still a good trail with virtually no signs of the dreaded washboard effect. At this point in your journey you will encounter a small wooden bridge that allows water to flow across both sides of the trail.

Rutland Railroad, Alburg, Vermont depot, 1967
[courtesy of Richard Symmes, Walker Transportation Collection of the Beverly Historical Society]

1.7 miles: Grade crossing for Route 78, as you exit the boundary of the refuge.

2.3 miles: Just beyond the treelines is a grassy area with an agricultural grade crossing to the fields on either side.

2.4 miles: You are entering some denser woods now as you come upon a fill. Coal droppings are found here also.

2.6 miles: Grade crossing of a paved road.

2.9 miles: Wide open and grass covered cinder. The nearby highway, Rte. 78, can be heard in the background.

3.2 miles: Grade crossing of a gravel road.

3.3 miles: You are in a cut here, and if observant, you will find some ties left over from days gone by. A house is on the left, as you are near the highway and entering East Alburg.

3.4 miles: Junction of the *wye-track*. This configuration was used at an interchange point to switch cars to another railroad's track or to turn locomotives to face the direction of travel. The left leg of the wye here led to the Central Vermont's mainline to Canada, which incidentally is only seven miles away. The right branch led to the C.V. trestle which crossed the lake and headed into Swanton, Vermont. The third leg of the wye is the mainline coming off the trestle into East Alburg and swinging north towards Canada. This is the only leg that is still in use today.

3.5 miles: The trail ends with either leg that you choose. Right comes out at the Trestle area, and the left side comes out facing north, just outside Alburg Springs on the CV mainline.

Central Vermont Railroad

1876.   At St. Albans, July 10th, 18

TIME TABLE — GOING SOUTH.

Mls.	STATIONS.	Pass.	Pass.	Pass.	Pass.
118	Rouse's Point......	4.35 "	8.00 am	3.50 "	12.15 pm
122	Alburgh...........	4.50 "	8.28 "	4.18 "	....
126	Alburgh Springs....	4.58 "	8.55 "	4.40 "	....
132	Swanton...........	5.14 "	9 35 "	5.10 "	....
142	**St. Albans**.... { Ar	5 35 "	10.40 "	6.00 "	....
	{ Lv	6.05 "	12.05 m	7.00 "	3.20 pm
147	North Georgia.....	6.18 "	12.15 pm	7.12 "	3.42 "
152	Georgia	6.28 "	12.25 "	7.24 "	4.00 "
155	Milton............	6.34 "	12.32 "	7.30 "	4.15 "
162	Colchester	6.50 "	12.48 "	7.45 "	4.45 "
166	Essex Junc......Ar	7 00 "	12.55 "	7.55 "	5 05 "
	Essex Junc......Lv	7.10 "	1.10 "	8.00 am	....
172	Winooski..........	7.22 "	1.23 "	8.14 "	....
174	**Burlington**... { Ar	7.30 "	1.30 "	8.20 "	....
	{ Lv	7 30 "	1.30 "	8.20 "	3.00 pm
181	Shelburne.........	7.42 "	1.42 "	8.35 "	3.15 "
186	Charlotte.........	7.53 "	1.52 "	8 48 "	3.29 "
190	No. Ferrisburg.....	8.02 "	2.00 "	8.57 "	3.39 "
193	Ferrisburg........	8.10 "	2.06 "	9.05 "	3.46 "
195	Vergennes.........	8.15 "	2.10 "	9.10 "	3.55 "
200	New Haven........	8.25 "	2.19 "	9.20 "	4.10 "
205	Brooksville.......	8.35 "	2.28 "	9.32 "	4.26 "
	Middlebury	8 42 "	2 32 "	9 42 "	4.37 "

CONDENSED TIME TABLE

Mls.	STATIONS.	Going South.	
	Ogdensburg Lv	†10.40 am	†6.00 p
25	Norwood	12.00 m	8.05
61	Malone.......... { Ar	1.42 pm	11.00
	{ Lv	1.47 "	2.35 a
103	Mooer's Junction........Lv	4.00 "	2.50
118	Rouse's Point...........	4.35 "	3.50
142	**St. Albans** { Ar	5.35 "	6.00
	{ Lv	6.05 "	7.00
166	Essex Junction	7.10 "	.....
174	Burlington..............	7.30 "	8.20
241	**Rutland**	10.00 "	11.05
270	Manchester, Vt	11.08 "	12.20 n
320	Troy, N.Y.	†2.45 am	2.25
324	Albany..................	1.00 "	2.40
352	Hudson	....	3 35
393	Poughkeepsie	3.42 "	4.50
466	New York, via Troy........Ar	6.30 "	7.00
262	**White River Junction**......	1.50 am	12.35
330	Concord.................	5.15 "	3.40
348	Manchester	6.15 "	4.22
363	Nashua...	6.55 "	5.05
403	**Boston**.................	8.35 "	6.37
409	Worcester	9.20 "	5.55

Rail-trail running through rural surroundings in northwestern Vermont (the Alburg Trail)

23 Burlington Waterfront Bikeway

Endpoints: Oakledge Park to Winooski River within the City of Burlington VT
Location: Chittenden County, City of Burlington, Vermont
Length: 7.3 miles
Surface: Asphalt

Uses:

To get there: Take I 89 to Exit 13. Follow this to the end at Route 7. Take Route 7 North for a short distance to Flynn Avenue on the left. Take Flynn Avenue to the end which is Oakledge Park. Park in the approved area and find the trail which is on the lakefront. The trail goes North which is to your right.
Contact:
Robert Whalen, Superintendent of Parks
Department of Parks and Recreation
1 LaValley Lane, Burlington, VT 05401
802-865-7247

Local resources for bike repairs/rentals:
Earl's Cycling & Fitness135 Main Street Burlington, VT.802-862-4203

In the 1950s, the Rutland Railroad experienced a resurgence in business due to the pro-active marketing and hands-on management style of Mr. Gardner Caverly. Traffic was getting back on the rails, and new diesels were bought to replace the aging and inefficient steam power. Things were looking up, but then Mr. Caverly retired in 1957 and a Mr. William I. Ginsberg took over. His experience was in the merchandising field, and he tried to apply his style of business to a railroad staffed with militant unions and anachronistic work rules of the steam era. On September 15, 1960 the unions walked out. Ordered back by the courts, the railroad operated during the one year cooling-off period. When the court-ordered decree expired on September 25, 1961, so did the Rutland. What ensued was the largest single abandonment in New England railroad history.

Most of the Rutland's route is still used today. The Vermont Railway runs from Bennington to Burlington. From Rutland to Bellows Falls, it is operated by the Green Mountain Railroad. The section from Burlington northward is now part ghost, visible only to the resolute explorer, or it is a Bikeway such as the one you are about to begin. Starting at Oakledge Park, it has all the facilities that you would normally expect, such as rest rooms and water fountains. As you get underway, the first thing you will notice is beautiful Lake Champlain. The lake is rarely out of view as the trail winds into downtown Burlington.

Lake Champlain and the Burlington skyline as viewed from the bikeway.

0.5 miles: The first interesting thing you come upon is Blanchard Beach. With its soft sand, small size, and being nearly deserted of people, it makes for a fine place to take in the sights.

0.6 miles: A tank farm and a cement wall on the beach.

0.7 miles: Crossing a bridge here which goes over a marshy area. This is not a bridge with any rail ancestry, but is notable for its unusual construction. Tennis courts and a residential neighborhood are next along the way.

0.8 miles: Harrison Avenue is approached now. You will be on this street for two blocks, then take a left when the Vermont Railway tracks are upon you. The bike trail now will be alongside the existing right-of-way for a while. The tracks are on the other side of a fence, so you don't have to worry about the safety of any small children in your party.

1.1 miles: Still alongside the VTRR tracks and now crossing a bridge which is over Lakeside Avenue. Industrial buildings in this area were once rail-served. The more modern of the two is The Blodgett Oven Company, maker of pizza ovens.

1.6 miles: Now you're going over a small bridge and passing a signal tower for the railroad, used to guard the approaches to the yard that lies just ahead.

23. Burlington Waterfront Bikeway

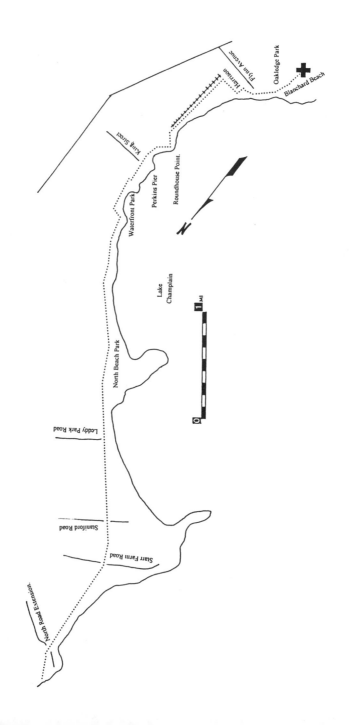

1.8 miles: You are now passing by Vermont Railway's headquarters and classification yard. The main building is a delightful, wood-sided structure that fits in with the Burlington ambiance of dignified charm. All administrative, dispatch, and operations functions are run out of this facility. The roundtable used for turning locomotives and the yard itself date back to the days of the old Rutland Railroad. This is a well-run and viable railroad with a positive future. The park here is known as Roundhouse Point.

2.0 miles: Passing by the City of Burlington's Water Pollution Control Plant. Also in this area is a marina which is part of the Roundhouse Point complex. It is called Perkins Pier. A city-owned & operated marina in Burlington Harbor, it has slips, moorings, and a launch area for trailerable boats. The trail will now zig-zag through the dock area, but is easily recognizable.

2.2 miles: Grade crossing at King Street, which has the ferry to New York.

2.3 miles: The big building you're now passing is the Union Station in Burlington. This was a passenger mecca for students and travelers for many years. Passenger trains no longer stop to board people, and the air walk over the tracks is demolished, but the building still retains its dignity and charm, and seems to be waiting for a new purpose.

2.4 miles: Grade crossing at the entrance to Burlington's Waterfront Park and Promenade. An old railroad signal tower is on the VTRR main-line in this area, but the main thing to see here is the nice park and waterfront activities. Amphitheater events include evening concerts and plays There is something else here that is not seen just anywhere: a giant kaleidoscope.

Dog-walker on the Burlington path

Signage on the Burlington Waterfront path

2.6 miles: Here is a pedestrian-crossing over the VTRR tracks heading north. There used to be a junction here between the Rutland's main line, which headed north, and the current track, which meets the Central Vermont Railway. Look for the old signal tower which protected the junction that is no longer here.

3.0 miles: You are leaving the urban area and entering a more rural setting.

3.4 miles: The trail starts to divert from the shore and climb up on the bluffs overlooking the lake.

3.9 miles: Now passing North Beach Park. Here you will find a 1,700-foot beach with lifeguards and picnic facilities. Camping for both tents and RVs is permitted. The access road to the park will pass underneath by going through a few culvert tubes.

4.3 miles: A bridge is overhead in this area as you go through a 40-foot deep cut. As the cut smooths out, you will still be in the forest but going uphill.

4.8 miles: Grade crossing at Driftwood Lane and its small residential community nearby.

4.9 miles: Grade crossing of a dirt road.

5.0 miles: Grade crossing for Leddy Park Road. This is Burlington's largest and most heavily used recreation facility. It features an 1800-foot beach, indoor ice rink, ball fields, nature trails, and playground.

5.2 miles: Grade crossing for Staniford Road. A residential neighborhood.

5.6 miles: Grade crossing for Starr Farm Road. Shortly after this is the Starr Farm Park / Bikepath Beach. A multi-purpose park with soccer fields, benches, and picnic tables.

6.0 miles: You are high above the lake now as you pass some exclusive condos with their "million dollar views."

7.0 miles: Grade crossing at North Road Extension.

7.1 miles: On a fill here with some houses nearby.

7.3 miles: The trail ends here on an bridge abutment that once carried the Rutland over the mouth of the Winooski River and on to the first of the Lake Champlain Islands, via the famous series of causeways and bridges.

Scenic Lake Champlain

24 Central Vermont Trail

Endpoints: St. Albans, Vermont, to Richford, Vermont
Location: Franklin County. Passing through the towns of St. Albans, Swanton, Fairfield, Sheldon, Enosburg, Berkshire, and Richford along the way.
Length: 24.7 miles
Surface: Original ballast, which here means large, sharp edged stones, approximately 2" in diameter. Vermont Route 105 basically parallels the trail, so you can get onto a good surface at any time your legs wear out. The construction season of 1995 will start a project to change this trail to a crushed limestone surface which will make the above warning not applicable.

Uses:

To get there: Take I 89 to Exit 20. At end of ramp go South on Route 7 until the intersection of Route 105, then go one more block and park in this general area where it is safe and approved. The trail starts here on the east side of Rte 7 and heads to the northeast. Look on the west side of the highway to find the end of the existing rail, and you'll be able to find the rail-trail across the street.

Contact:
Charles Vile, Trails Coordinator
Department of Parks and Recreation
111 West Street
Essex Junction, VT 05452
802-879-6565

Mr. Stan Beauregard, Chairperson
Central Vermont Rail-trail Council
P.O. Box 1
St. Albans, VT 05478
1-802-524-2965

Local resources for bike repairs/rentals:
At time of publication, none found in the area.
Burlington might be the nearest point.

St. Albans has an interesting history; it was the site of the northernmost raid of the Confederate forces during the Civil War. On October 19, 1864, Lt. Bennet Young led a contingent of about twenty soldiers on a raid of the town. Two banks lost more than $200,000, and livery stables in town lost horses, saddles, etc. One person was killed and two wounded in the guerrilla-style hit-and-run attack. The Confederate forces escaped by way of a plank road that led to Canada. That plank road eventually became the right-of-way of the Central Vermont Railway's Richford Branch, the site of this trail.

The Central Vermont Railway (CV) was a subsidiary of the Canadian National Railroad and had its headquarters at St. Albans for over 100 years. In early 1995 the CV was sold and is now known as The New England Central Railroad, a subsidiary of the short line railroad company Rail-Tex. This railroad is generally a straight-through line with no major branches in its property from the Canadian border above Lake Champlain to the Long Island Sound at New London, Connecticut. No major branches existed after the demise of the Richford Branch in 1984.

The Richford Branch served a straight forward purpose; to connect with the Canadian Pacific Railroad (CPR) at the border-town of Richford, Vermont. CPR had a major customer here, H.K. Webster Co. Inc. (Blue Seal Feeds) that shipped many boxcars of feed and other food-stuffs. The Central Vermont also had rights to switch the plant through a reciprocal switch agreement. The local production of milk meant another ready customer for the CV. This traffic remained steady until the onset of the trucking industry and the now ubiquitous ten-wheeled, stainless-steel tankers.

The CV ran this line in spite of declining traffic until a derailment on the bridge over the Missisquoi River at Sheldon Junction in June of 1984. This accident, along with the demise of interchange traffic with the St. Johnsbury and Lamoille County Railroad at Sheldon Junction, determined that this line would never again be profitable. After the rails were pulled out in the early 1990s, the State of Vermont took over management of the site as a multi-use path. It is very popular as a snowmobile trail.

At the northern terminus in Richford, the trail will offer a potential connection to trails in Canada, beginning across the border in Sutton. These trails were under construction in the fall of 1994 and should be completed in the summer of 1995. Long-range plans call for a network of hundreds of kilometers of trails eventually reaching Montreal.

Enjoy this truly historic and international trail.

24. Central Vermont Trail

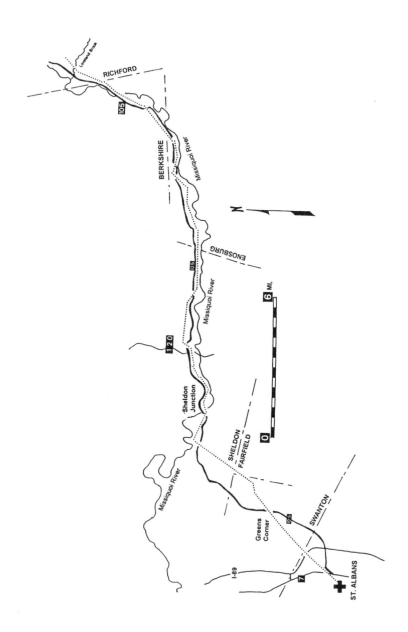

0.2 miles: On the left through the trees is the Eveready Battery Plant, an on-line customer until shortly after the derailment that shut the line down in this area.

0.5 miles: Interstate 89 passes over the trail here as you exit the community of St. Albans and enter into the town of Swanton.

1.4 miles: A culvert over a small stream is here. A sample of the picturesque vistas that lay ahead.

2.3 miles: Here is the first of many grade crossings of Route 105, a constant companion of yours and an outlet to an easier ride if the ballast gets to be to tiresome. This area is known as Greens Corner and has another small stream to cross. In the period around the First World War, there was a creamery here owned by H.P. Hood, situated on the southwest side of the highway crossing.

3.6 miles: Grade crossing of a small country road as you skirt the corner of the town of Fairfield and enter into the town of Sheldon.

4.1 miles: Crossing over the small country road again as you go between two small hills.

4.7 miles: Grade crossing of another rural lane as you go past a trucking terminal and a residential neighborhood and cross the highway again. Off to the left beyond the truck staging area was another large on line customer. Boise Cascade used to get many cars here in the manufacture of paper, both inbound and outbound.

Ex-dairy products transfer building

Overgrown and unused diamond at Sheldon Junction

5.5 miles: On a fill now as you go past some small pastures.

5.7 miles: Grade crossing of a driveway that leads to a farm off to the left. A concrete culvert is here and the highway comes back into proximity again.

6.0 miles: Grade crossing at 105 again, with a slight detour; you must use the highway bridge across the Missisquoi River because the rail bridge has one span knocked out. This happened on June 29, 1984, when a combined Canadian Pacific-Boston & Maine train operating on the Central Vermont, derailed and damaged the east span. Courts held that the B&M was responsible to pay for damages to the bridge, but it was never repaired.

6.6 miles: Go past the convenience store and turn right at the access road to the industry. Here is Sheldon Junction, site of the diamond and interchange point with the St. Johnsbury and Lamoille County Railroad. The industrial complex here has an interesting history. This was originally a Hood Milk Creamery from 1924 to 1941. It was sold to Ralston Purina which ran a feed distribution business until the Boudreau Bros. took it over for the manufacture of fertilizers, in 1967. The tracks of the St. J&LC are still in place but are not used at the present time. Interestingly, the junction here with the St. J&LC provided a way to get service to the Richford end when the bridge just west of here was first knocked out of service. This routing only lasted a few weeks when it was cancelled and the line to Richford finally abandoned. In the early years of the junction there was a passenger station here at the southwest corner. This structure include extensive wooden platforms, and a water tank here provided water for the steam engines of both roads.

8.4 miles: The river is close by and you are going past the scenic River Farm.

8.7 miles: Going past another restaurant/snack-bar establishment.

9.4 miles: Grade crossing of a small road. This is near the intersection of Routes 120 and 105. The small road leads to a bridge over the Missisquoi River and into the village of Sheldon.

9.6 miles: Grade crossing of Rte 105 again. You are now on the north side of the highway.

10 miles: If you are here in the summer, you'll be passing a sea of corn fields.

11.4 miles: Grade crossing of Rte 236.

11.6 miles: Grade crossing of Rte 105. Once again you are between the river and the road.

Small timber trestle that carries only memories of trains today.

12.0 miles: On the left, a beautiful brick farmhouse with an interesting slate roof.

12.2 miles: Lovely vistas of rolling meadows.

13.3 miles: Agricultural grade crossing.

13.6 miles: Parent Riverside Farm is found here with its well-kept buildings.

14.6 miles: Grade crossing of 105 once again as you are entering the town of Enosburg. Lavalley's Service Center is here for a rest stop or a drink. In the years prior to the depression, this town had two creameries as well as a packing house; all disappeared now.

14.8 miles: Small bent-timber type bridge that crosses a small brook.

16.0 miles: You're in the middle of an open valley here with some stands of cedar trees nearby.

17.3 miles: Here are some views of the quintessential rural Vermont lifestyle.

17.6 miles: Grade crossing of Rte 105 again and some ancient ties are visible in this area, probably leftovers from the scrapping operation.

17.7 miles: The Dairy Center with a restaurant and bar complex.

18.6 miles: Crossing 105 once again and then a small culvert, followed by a crossing of Long Road.

19.2 mile: Agricultural grade crossing as you pass a dairy farm.

19.4 miles: Grade crossing of Rte 105 again as the Missisquoi River meanders closeby and then veers away.

19.8 miles: Here is a run-down building along the tracks that must have been used in the transfer of milk and other diary products to the railroad. Built with metal sheathing, it is in very bad condition today but it gives an impression of the construction of this type of building.

19.9 miles: Grade crossing of 105 once again as you pass the Lazy A Farm and enter into the township of Berkshire.

20.2 miles: A stand of woods are nearby as you pass the center of activity in the town of East Berkshire and then cross over the highway again.

20.6 miles: Grade crossing for agricultural equipment; then a small culvert.

21.0 miles: Grade crossing a small country road.

21.9 miles: Grade crossing of River Run Road, and then the biggest bridge that is rideable on the trail. A through-truss type, it crosses the Missisquoi River. A dirt road is found at the east end of the span.

22.4 miles: Grade crossing a dirt road.

23.1 miles: Another quaint dairy farm is here with its modern, blue, steel silo.

23.5 miles: Passing into the town of Richford.

24.1 miles: Crossing Loveland Brook via a bridge with its original wooden timber deck and the crossing of a dirt road.

24.3 miles: Passing by another dairy farm as the end of the trail is near.

24.7 miles: End of the trail in the town of Richford. Take a left at this paved road and you'll reach Route 105 in few hundred yards. On the way you'll pass by what used to be the station and interchange yard with the Canadian Pacific Railroad. Taking a right will lead you to the CP and its active track.

BOSTON OFFICE, CENTRAL VERMONT R.R. LINE,

22 Washington Street, 322

HOCKING, Freight Agt.　　　**T. EDWARD BOND, Ticket Agt.**

F. L. PARKER, Chief Clerk.

25 Delaware and Hudson Rail-Trail

Endpoints: Castleton State College, Castleton, Vermont, to the New York border at West Rupert, Vermont
Location: Bennington and Rutland Counties. Runs between Castleton and Poultney in the Northern section, and West Pawlet and West Rupert in the Southern section.
Length: 20 miles in Vermont already developed; an additional 14 miles in New York not yet developed.
Surface: Gravel and original cinder ballast.

Uses:

To get there: *Northern Section:* Out of Rutland take Route 4.west to 4A, which is exit 6. Follow this west to Castleton and take a left at South Street which leads to the State College at Castleton. Parking is available about 1/2 mile down on the left behind the school security office, near the observatory building. *Southern Section:* Follow Rte. 30 North out of Manchester, VT to Rte 153; then to Rte 315 into West Pawlet VT. At the center of town you can park across the street from Duchie's General Store.

Contact:
Gary Salmon, Trails Coordinator, Dept. of Forests, Parks and Recreation
Vermont Agency of Natural Resources
RFD 2 Box 2161
Pittsford, VT 05763
802-483-2314

Local resources for bike repairs/rentals:
Battenkill Sports Bicycle Shop, Manchester Center, 802-362-2734

This trail is among our favorites because it has beautiful vistas of dairy farms with meadows rising on the foothills of the Green Mountain National Forest and forgotten towns unspoiled by the 20th century, where the whole town comes out to see the Fourth of July Parade, sip lemonade, and watch the gawking tourists. These are places where the local activities once centered around the railroad and the depots on line.

This railroad was built because this area had the country's highest quality and most sought-after slate for building construction. In the 1840s, when it became apparent just how big the veins of slate and marble were, the railroad was seen as a savior to bring these heavy commodities to market. This railroad ran from Castleton to Eagle Bridge where it connected with the line to Troy, New York, a port city on the Hudson River. To get there, the surveyors had to snake back and forth across the border twice. When mentioned in official circles, it was known as the Rutland and Washington Division of the Delaware and Hudson Railroad. To the locals and the rail crews it was known as the "Slate Picker."

By the 1880s the slate business was booming and there were 53 manufacturers in Rutland County shipping 250 cars a month to virtually every area of the country. The eventual decline of the slate business was in part due to the decline of the railroad. As you travel the trail, you will notice that there are many piles of tailings containing gray, purple, green, and red slate. Some of the country roads in the area are also paved with the waste. It makes for an unusual sight. The slate business is not totally gone, for there are still a few such operations to be seen. The passenger service from Castleton to Salem was discontinued in 1934. Other commodities, such as milk, prospered through the railroads until the 1950s when the refrigerator truck came onto the scene. The last years of the line saw a shift in the flow of traffic to mostly inbound traffic and the Slate Picker ran only as needed. Service was discontinued in 1983 and the state of Vermont tried to find an acceptable shortline operator. They were unsuccessful and by 1990-91 the rails and ties were removed and the trail upgraded to its current status.

Cinder based path in the early stages of the D&H Trail

25. Delaware & Hudson
Recreation Trail

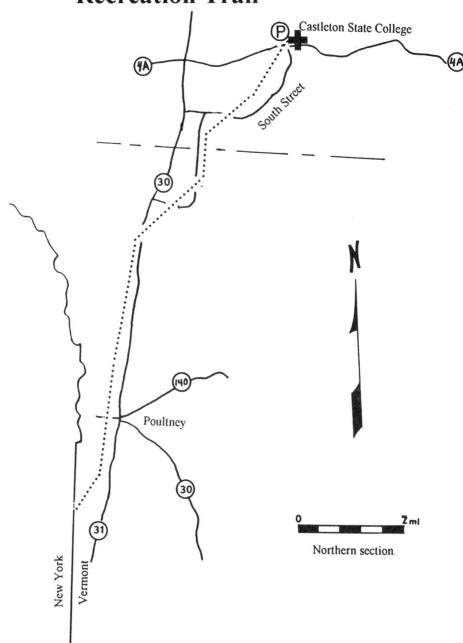

Castleton State College

4A

South Street

30

140

Poultney

30

31

New York

Vermont

N

0   2 mi

Northern section.

0.0 miles: The trail starts in the college parking lot by the observatory and heads South. You will see the cinder and gravel path. This school is attended by over 2000 students, so the trail gets used by many who enjoy the outdoors.

0.1 miles: Grade crossing of South Street. About 1/10th mile past here is the remains of a wye track which turned trains and serviced the Staso/Castleton Quarry which is still in operation.

0.3 miles: The road bed widens out in this area and you are on a bit of a fill.

0.7 miles: Still on the fill, the area opens to reveal the beautiful Vermont pasture lands with a farm in the distance.

1.1 miles: A road approaches on the right and within 1/10 mile it turns into a grade crossing.

1.4 miles: A grade crossing for a farm.

1.6 miles: A bridge over South Street. This is a decked bridge with all pressure treated timbers and a five-foot railing on the side installed for safety.

1.8 miles: Passing over a grade crossing for a private road.

2.5 miles: Another dirt road grade crossing and into some woods again.

2.8 miles: Out of the woods now; the road bed is lined with wild raspberries.

2.9 miles: Grade crossing of Lewis Road. Footings of an old mill are visible here along with the tailings pile of an old slate mill, the Lucky Strike Quarry.

3.2 miles: Grade crossing of Walker Road which leads to a few farm houses.

3.8 miles: A pond is here with a bridge over the feeder stream at the south end. The depth is increased by a beaver dam on the left.

4.0 miles: Going through a bit of a cut with gentle earth sides. Around this area there are some abandoned old railroad telegraph poles. Though they are missing their insulators and wires, they do remind you of what was once here.

4.1 miles: Grade crossing of Rte. 30 which is a busy highway so be careful. The big abutments in this area were part of an original highway alignment which was discontinued in the 1950s.

4.6 miles: You are on another fill in this area which is about fifteen feet above the surrounding farms and has a commanding view of the countryside.

4.9 miles: An agricultural grade crossing is here.

5.2 miles: On a fill again with open pastures on each side. The sensation is one of being on a dike with a green ocean on each side.

6.3 miles: Out of the woods and on a 15-ft.-high fill. There used to be a slate dust mill here that made products for tennis courts and various paint pigments.

6.7 miles: Everyone's pastoral vision of Vermont: a farm and barn with the obligatory silo aged a weather-beaten gray. This is in the town of Poultney on Route 30. On the other side of the trail is a baseball field which can be lit up for night games.

7.2 miles: Going by a trucking terminal which is fairly new and is built near the site of a Hood Milk creamery which burned down in the late 1970s.

Through the woods of western Vermont

7.3 miles: Entering the Town of Poultney proper, the railroad ran right through the center of town. This was because the town was moved to meet the railroad which was arriving at a slightly different location from the original town. East Poultney is the original Poultney. Here you can grab a bite to eat and relax along with a visit to some delightful shops, one of which is a bookstore in the old freight station. The old passenger station is now an antique shop and some of the other old rail-served industrial buildings have been converted to modern uses. This is a typical New England practice; to maintain the integrity of the structure, yet adapt it to more practical uses. You will see this all over town. Use caution as you'll be on city streets.

7.8 miles: A relatively long bridge (80 feet) which crosses a wide slow stream, the Poultney River. The Staso/Hampton Quarry's switch was near here and the track is in the weeds. This quarry is still active.

8.1 miles: This bridge over a small stream with lily pads for decoration.

9.2 miles: Another slate quarry is on the left with its tell-tale tailings pile and "stick" crane. This is the still active Western Slate Quarry ,also called McCarthy Quarry, in operation since the 1840s. The *Northern Section* of the trail ends here.

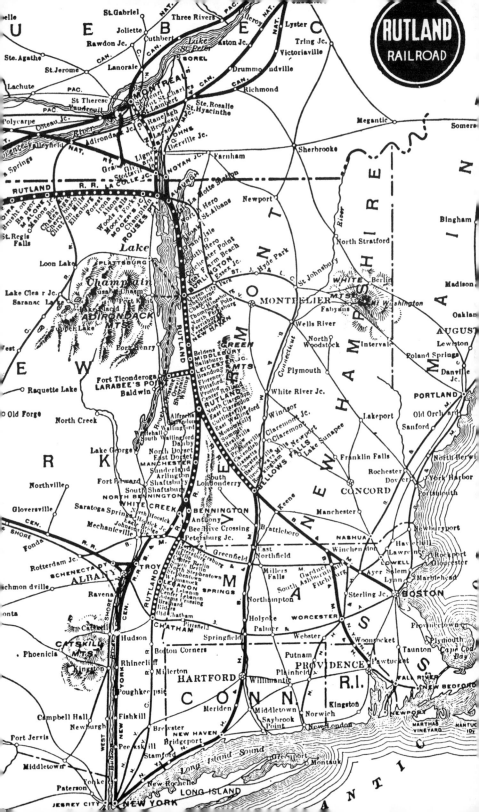

25. Delaware & Hudson Recreation Trail

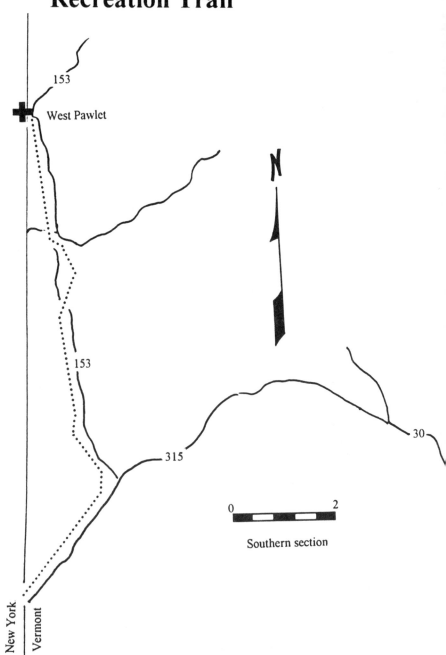

153

West Pawlet

153

315

30

N

0   2

Southern section

New York

Vermont

When you begin the Southern section at the West Pawlet center area, you'll find an old D&H freight house still standing at the center of activity in this quaint old town. There is also another vacant building from the past in this town, an abandoned Chevrolet dealership that was obviously built in the twenties. The ubiquitous general store, Duchie's Store, is a fine place to meet people and to grab a couple of sodas for the ride ahead. Standing at Duchie's store and looking across the street at the D&H freight depot, the border with New York is only 100 yards to the left. The D&H Recreation Trail starts at the depot and heads off south to the right.

0.0 miles: As soon as you go past the abandoned Chevy dealership you'll be coming upon a bridge which is 112-feet long and crosses over the Indian River which will be meandering back and forth along the trail.
0.1 miles: Another bridge, this time a through-truss type. At 88 feet long, it is somewhat rare and is nicely decked with pressure-treated timbers. The sound of the birds provide the only fanfare of your passage in this rural area. There is an old wooden marker here, reminiscent of the days of the steam locomotive.
0.2 miles: You now come upon the old mill complex that was once known as the Vermont Milk and Cream Co. From here, hundreds of insulated boxcars of milk were shipped each year primarily to the New York market.

Ex-Vermont Milk & Cream Complex

Old Delaware & Hudson Railway Freight Depot in West Pawlet.

0.3 miles: Open fields belonging to the Cramer Farm where there is also a Maple sugar house.

0.4 miles: A culvert now crosses under the trail.

0.5 miles: An agricultural grade crossing with corn fields on each side.

1.1 miles: Passing through a long corn field.

1.9 miles: Another agricultural grade crossing between farm fields.

2.1 miles Grade crossing of a dirt road; the trail goes into the woods.

2.3 miles: Grade crossing of a paved road, Route 153, a State highway which may be busy, so use caution.

2.4 miles: Stream is once again nearby and on the right.

2.5 miles: Grade crossing of another dirt road. The trail is now grass-covered.

2.6 miles: Small wooden bridge over the always present Indian River.

3.1 miles: Corn fields to your right with open fields to the left. Here also is a small wooden bridge.

3.5 miles: In the forest again with a canopy of leaves.

3.6 miles: Abutments for a bridge that at one time crossed over the railroad.

3.7 miles: Grade crossing of Route 153 again. Watch for cars because they will not be expecting to see you in this area.

4.0 miles: Grade crossing of a dirt road paved with tailings from the local quarry industry. An abandoned barn is located here.

4.3 miles: Another wooden marker that denotes the miles from the next major division point. This one says "EB28"-Eagle Bridge 28 miles.

*Restored Depot
in Poultney, Vermont:
Converted to modern uses
and prospering again.*

4.5 miles: Corn fields and another wooden bridge.

5.1 miles: Farm house off to the left has an interesting slate patterned roof.

5.5 miles: Another wooden bridge and also a slate tailings pile.

5.8 miles: The trail opens up wider on a fill of cinder ballast. The pasture land on each side is about 8 feet below and affords a good view of the surroundings.

6.3 miles: Going down-grade now, approaching a small pond which is on the right and Route 153 is on your immediate left.

6.5 miles: Marsh off to the right and an access point here to get to Route 153.

6.8 miles: Another "typical" Vermont scene with farms and vine-covered silos.

7.1 miles: Small community of Rupert with the essential white church for a centerpiece. Nearby is the Rupert Depot which once served as a combination passenger station and freight depot. Most of the freight here was milk going out-bound to the market. The concrete footing across the trail from the depot is evidence there was once a water tank for servicing the steam locomotives.

7.7 miles: Picturesque view of weeping willows and farm houses with a backdrop of grazing cows on the hillsides before the Taconic Mountains.

8.6 miles: An interesting deck bridge with a catwalk cantilevered off to one side. This one also crosses the Indian River which has followed us for so long. Here also can be seen another example of a recycled industrial building.

8.9 miles: Down-grade again with the stream still our companion and into another glade of woods.

9.2 miles: Out of the woods and upon another grade crossing of a dirt road.

9.5 miles: Passing two agricultural grade crossings.

9.6 miles: The Vermont section ends here at the border with New York, where a granite marker can be seen denoting the boundary. It is not recommended to continue on the trail in New York because it is privately owned and trespassers are not welcomed.

26 Montpelier and Wells River Trail

Endpoints: Rte 302, Groton, Vermont, to Winooski River area of Marshfield, Vermont, within the Groton State Forest.
Location: Caledonia County, Vermont, towns of Groton and Marshfield.
Length: 13.2 miles
Surface: Gravel and original ballast

Uses:

To get there: I-91 to exit 17, then follow Route 302 west for approximately eight miles, then turn right onto Route 232. Go about one mile and you'll see Ricker Mills Road on the left. Park on the right at the foot of Ricker Pond.
Contact:
Dave Willard, Trail Coordinator
Vermont Department of Natural Resources
184 Portland Street
St. Johnsbury, VT 05819
802-748-8787
Local resources for bike repairs/rentals:
Onion River Sports, 20 Langdon Street, Montpelier, 802-229-9409
Onion River Sports, 395 N. Main Street, Barre, 802 476-9750

The Montpelier & Wells River Railroad (M&WR) was chartered in 1867 with a mandate to build a line between those two communities and the connecting railroads there. At Montpelier, this was the Central Vermont Railroad and at Wells River, this meant a junction with the Connecticut River Railroad, now best known as the Boston & Maine Railroad. The line wasn't finished until late 1873; regular passenger and freight service began at that time. In 1888, the Barre Railroad was formed under the control of the M&WR, with the intention of providing economical transportation for the vast granite quarries at Barre, which is near Montpelier. With the completion of the 20-odd miles of mainline and spurs in 1889, the Barre Railroad began moving thousands of cars of architectural and monumental granite to points all across the country.

The vast amount of traffic being generated here was being noticed by the big railroads and the financiers who controlled them. In 1911, the Boston & Maine Railroad took control of the M&WR and provided necessary operational improvements and financial stability.

In 1925 the B & M passed control of the Vermont subsidiary to a local board of directors. It was felt that local management could provide a hands-on management style that would impress the shippers and restore confidence in the line. This formula of "local management" is used today in the reasoning behind the large Class 1 railroads "spinning off" branch lines. This practice is attracting much interest and press today, as it is responsible for the resurgence and profitability of today's railroads. It is interesting that this concept was first tried out in Vermont in 1925.

In the 1920s and 30s, however, this kind of management was doomed to failure because of the inability to address the increasingly archaic work-rules of the operating unions, and the erosion of the core-traffic-base caused by the burgeoning trucking industry. In 1955 the ICC was petitioned to abandon the entire line. It was noted that the revenue from the Montpelier to Wells River section represented 5% of the total, while this area represented 40% of the maintenance costs of the railroad. Just prior to final approval for abandonment, the owners of the line entered into negotiations with Samuel Pinsly of Boston for the sale of the railroad.

Sam Pinsly was the original short-line entrepreneur. By the mid 1950s, he had made quite a name for himself. His first railroad, the Hoosac Tunnel & Wilmington Railroad on the Massachusetts-Vermont border, was obtained in 1937. Some of his later New England acquisitions included the Sanford & Eastern in Maine and the Concord & Claremont in New Hampshire. (A component of the Concord & Claremont is the *Sugar River Recreation Trail.*)

With regards to the M & WR, Pinsly made it clear that he did not want to buy the maintenance nightmare section from Montpelier to the Wells River interchange with the Boston and Maine. He only wanted the area of the granite quarries from Barre to Montpelier, and would expand the connection at Montpelier with the Central Vermont Railroad, forever severing the B&M link. The ICC and the State of Vermont agreed, and the Montpelier and Barre Railroad came into being in December 1956. The section east of Montpelier, the subject of this chapter, was torn out the following spring, and the right of way sold to the Vermont Parks and Forests Department, who in turn transferred large sections east of Rickers to the Highway Department for highway realignment.

This is a fun trail in mid-state Vermont that has a pleasant rural flavor and some spectacular mountain scenery along the way. Enjoy the trip!

26. Montpelier and Wells River Trail

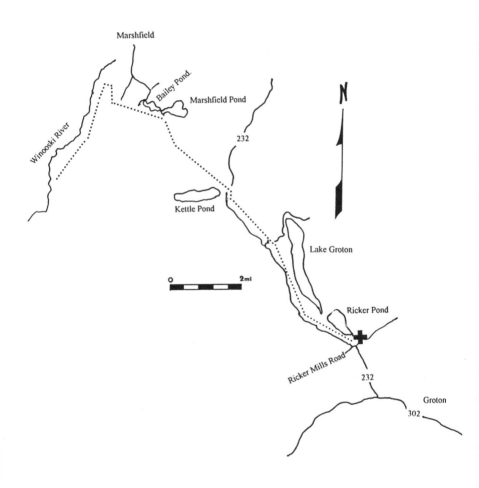

Marshfield

Bailey Pond.

Marshfield Pond

Winooski River

232

Kettle Pond

N

Lake Groton

2mi

Ricker Pond

Ricker Mills Road

232

Groton

302

0.0 miles: At the start you'll be going by Ricker Pond which is part of the campground and park complex of Groton State Forest. A picturesque small dam is on the south end of the pond. The trail in this initial area is wide and smooth and there are a couple of private docks for small boats. Interestingly, this area at Rickers was the site of the reputedly longest running sawmill operation in the United States, from 1790-1965.

0.2 miles: As you enter the park complex proper, you'll see some branches off the trail. These lead to hiking paths and picnic areas in the park. Comfort facilities are here and open in the summer months.

0.8 miles: The trail diverges from the park maintenance road, which shares the initial stages here. The surface is an open grass-centered path. The route of the rail-trail is the one with the metal gate as a barrier. Occasional ties are seen here which is a surprise because the rails were pulled out in the mid-50s.

1.1 miles: On a hillside with the lower side to the right as you head north.

1.2 miles: This area was known as Lakeside Station. This was a flag-stop type station, where passengers wanting to board the next passenger train, would hang a flag from the small shelter to signal the train to stop. Also here was a passing siding, to allow trains to double-up over the hill. This means that heavy or long trains from Wells River, would be cut in half to make the steep grade here, parked on this siding, and the second section would be brought up to join and continue on to Montpelier. Today the "Depot Brook Trail" intersection is here. This is one of Vermont's vast networks of snowmobile paths. A sign is here pointing out the various services for the hardy winter enthusiast.

1.3 miles: A stream is crossed here that comes down from the mountain on the left to the valley below on the right. A small bridge facilitates the stream. Another dirt road or trail crosses the path.

1.5 miles: Canopy of trees overhead provide shelter from the sun and make for interesting shadows.

1.8 miles: A beautiful waterfall comes down the hillside and crosses under the trail.

2.1 miles: Up-grade here as the right side drops off.

2.4 miles: Gigantic cascade of boulders is on the left. Lake Groton is becoming more visible in the valley down to the right.

2.8 miles: Continuing to climb the grade as the canopy of trees has thinned.

3.1 miles: Granite marker, but any writing on it has been obliterated.

3.3 miles: Branch off to the right leads down to the lake and private campgrounds.

3.6 miles: Grade crossing of a paved road. This is an access road to the lake and more private campgrounds.

4.0 miles: This is an open area with a good view of the mountains on the right. Owls Head, Little Deer, and Big Deer Mountains are the foremost ones.

4.4 miles: Another open area here shows signs of a logging operation.

Ubiquitous silo and mile marker (EB= Eagle Bridge and A=Albany)

4.8 miles: Small cut and another logging operation is here along with some more splendid views of the neighboring mountains.

5.2 miles: A bridge here is built out of 4x10s vertically laid in place on top of the original girders. This is wider than the primary design so that it can support passing snowmobiles. A pleasant waterfall is here also.

This is Stillwater Brook, which is fed from Kettle Pond on the left, a few hundred yards into the woods.

5.5 miles: Grade crossing of Route 232. This is a busy road, so do use caution when crossing because the cars may not be expecting to see you. When you cross, you'll come upon a relatively steep down-grade and then a correspondingly sharp up-grade. A bridge or overpass may have been here at one time. An open area here is allowing you to see Burnt Mountain and Marshfield Mountain up close along with a small pond.

6.1 miles: Basically flat or even a little down-grade here while the smell of the balsam and other soft woods make for a pleasant section.

6.3 miles: Into an area of meadows and bucolic Vermont scenery.

7.0 miles: Open area with some young trees and an occasional culvert.

7.5 miles: The basic layout of the land is still down to the right and up to the left. The trail shows signs of cinder base in this area.

7.9 miles: Access roads are here that lead to Marshfield Pond and Bailey Pond. A sign saying "Edgewater M&WR" has been installed by a resident and made to look like a railroad station sign.

8.2 miles: Marshes on the right have bird houses on stands in the water.

8.7 miles: Fork in the trail is here. Take the left one as that is the railroad bed. The one to the right is an access road to the ponds.

8.9 miles: Down-grade and curve to the right, then a sharp turn to the left and south.

9.1 miles: Back into the dense canopy of woods.

9.7 miles: Fork in the trail here. Take the left fork. You'll find a gate that blocks access to cars that normally may be found on parts of the trail.

10.0 miles: Going past a small fill that is 12-20 feet tall. Basically sandy here and curving to the left as you go uphill. This area is the big hook in the trail.

10.2 miles: A big hill with a drop-off to the right, a sharp incline to the left.

10.8 miles: Clearing here with some logging roads on the right and another fill coming up. Still bending slightly to the left.

11.0 miles: A small cut is encountered with pines and birches here.

11.1 miles: Logging road is on the right and another fill follows.

11.2 miles: Ramshackle remains of a house, along with some ties and tie-plates remaining from the scrapping operation of 1956-57.

11.3 miles: Another ramshackle house is here.

11.4 miles: Logging road access points are in this area.

11.5 miles: This cut is a little higher on the right and about 10 feet deep.

12.2 miles: Swampy area with ties used to help hold the bed in place.

12.6 miles Logging clearing is here.

12.9 miles: On another fill again. This one is approximately 15 feet high.

13.2 miles: A fork in the trail here signals the end of the rail-trail. The Winooski River is nearby on the right, and some trees are down on the trail to prevent anyone from going any further.

MAINE CENTRAL RAILROAD

RAIL AIR BUS SERVICE

A COMPLETE TRANSPORTATION SERVICE

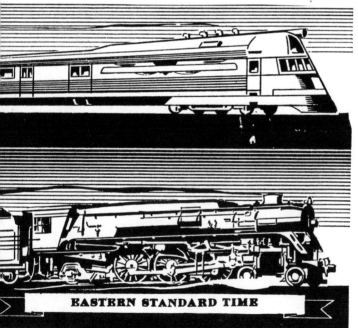

EASTERN STANDARD TIME

REVISED TO JAN. 5, 1937

Appendix:

Glossary, Resources, Maps and Books

Glossary of Terms

BALLAST: Rocks, usually about 2-3 inches in diameter placed below the ties and track area to facilitate drainage of water away from the track and also to prevent the growth of weeds.

CINDER: The refuse of burnt coal. This was used in the construction of some fills and sometimes was used as ballast or road construction.

CUT: An excavation in the ground to maintain the gentle slope required of a railroad.

FILL: An area raised to be above the surrounding ground to maintain the gentle grade. The material used in a fill is usually from a nearby cut.

GRADE: A term used to describe the degree of change from level. Railroads were usually not able to climb grades steeper than 5 %; i.e., a five-foot rise for every one hundred feet of travel. It is rare to see any gradient steeper than 2.5% on an old railroad line listed in this book.

GRADE CROSSING: This is where a road crossed the tracks at the same level. Busier crossings usually had the protection of gates which lowered to block the automobiles. Some areas warranted a grade crossing watch-man who came out to manually put down the gate and prevent the cars from crossing.

ROAD (S): Short for railroad, for example the New Haven road.

TIES: Wooden timbers usually 8.5-feet-long, used to support and maintain the gauge of the rails.

Basic overview of railroad bridges common to the Northeast

There are two basic categories that apply here.
(A) **Deck Type** structures which have the supporting members underneath the bridge.
(B) **Through Type** structures have the supporting members bestride or over the track.

These categories are further broken down by the following widespread models. (1) **Girder** (steel). Usually made up of separate section riveted with plates and angles to make for a strong but generally short bridge. (2) **Beam** (wood). Early bridges were commonly constructed of wood timbers. (3) **Truss** (wood or steel). A series of structural shapes fashioned into an open system that are generally variations of the letter "W." Wooden versions of this were often covered to prevent exposure to the elements, hence 'covered bridges.'

Other variations of bridges and their definitions

Trestle: A series of short bridges that are individually supported along the length.

Viaduct: Generally a stone structure that spans a wide valley.

Culvert: A pipe or box that is back filled with dirt and gravel.

RAILROAD NAME ABBREVIATIONS

B & A; Boston & Albany Railroad
B&M; Boston & Maine Railroad
CLCO; Claremont & Concord Railroad
CN; Canadian National Railway
CNE; Central of New England
CP; Canadian Pacific Railroad
CR; Conrail
CV; Central Vermont Railway
D&H; Delaware & Hudson Railroad
GTI; Guilford Transportation Industries
MEC; Maine Central Railroad
M&WR; Montpelier & Wells River Railroad
NECR; New England Central Railroad
NH or **NY, NH&H;** The New York, New Haven and Hartford Railroad.
NYC; New York Central Railroad
NY&NE; New York & New England Railroad
PC; Penn-Central
PT Co.; Portland Terminal Railroad Company
RUT; Rutland Railroad
St. J&LC; St. Johnsbury and Lamoille County Railroad
SR&RL; Sandy River & Rangeley Lakes Railroad
VTRR; Vermont Railroad

Sources for Maps, Books, Organizations

Maps and Atlases

Available road maps and atlases of New England are too numerous to make a complete listing here. However, bookshops or outfitters will have an abundant supply of local publications to help you find your way to the trails mentioned in this book. It is a good idea to obtain the appropriate map or atlas for the trail area you expect to visit. (Spend your valuable free time on the trail, not on the road trying to find it.) The USGS topographic maps (known as "topos" or "quads") are useful for exploring these trails in the field. Consult the yellow pages under Maps/Dealers to obtain these useful government publications. They cost about $4.00 each. USGS dealers tend to carry only those maps of their local general area. (If you live in Connecticut, don't expect a dealer to stock topos of Maine. Its best to call ahead and ask about availability.)

DeLorme Mapping Company
P.O. Box 298, Freeport, Maine 04032 (207-865-4171)
This company makes a series of Atlases covering the states of northern New England; Vermont, New Hampshire, and Maine. Their New Hampshire map is particularly valuable because it shows abandoned railroad lines. Each one of the series has sections on conventional bicycle routes, canoeing, fishing, hiking, museums, and historic sites. They are a bargain at $11.95-to-$14.95. None are available as yet for Massachusetts, Connecticut, or Rhode Island. For these areas the Rand McNally County-based series is recommended, or similar ones such as the Jimapco Company's or Champion. All of these show railroad lines (usually the abandoned ones also) along with street names.

DeLorme Mapping also offers a CD ROM for home computers called *Street Atlas USA*. This is an almost indispensible tool for finding any point in the continental U.S., and it retails for about $75. With search tools based on names, zip codes, or zoom-in, this program prints maps in any scale that you need.

Sources for USGS Topographic Maps

New England Cartographics
P.O. Box 9369, North Amherst, MA 01059 (413-549-4124)

United States Geological Survey
Box 23286, Federal Center, Bldg. 41, Denver, CO 80223

Books

Beauregard, Mark W. *Railroad Stations of New England Today: Vol. 1, The Boston & Maine Railroad,* Railroad Avenue Enterprises, Inc. (1979), P.O. Box 114, Flanders, New Jersey 07836.

Belcher, C. Francis. *Logging Railroads of the White Mountains,* Appalachian Mountain Club, Boston, Massachusetts (1980).

Boston & Maine Historical Society, Inc. *The Central Mass.* (1975).
The last word on the ill-fated, third east-west railroad through Massachusetts.

Farson, Robert H. *Cape Cod Railroads, Including Martha's Vineyard and Nantucket,* Cape Cod Historical Publications (1993), Box 281, Yarmouth Port, Massachusetts, 02675.

Jones, Robert C. *The Central Vermont Railway,* Sundance Publications (1981), P.O. Box 597, Silverton, Colorado 81433.

----------------- *Railroads of Vermont,* New England Press (1993), P.O. Box 575, Shelburne, VT 05482.

Jones, Robert. *The Boston & Maine:Three Colorful Decades of New England Railroading,* Trans-Anglo Books (1991) P.O. Box 6444, Glendale CA 91225.

Jordan, Philip R. *Rails Beyond the Rutland,* Carstens Publications, Inc. (1988), P. O. Box 700, Newton, NJ 07860-0700.

Karr, Ronald Dale. *Lost Railroads of New England,* Branch Line Press (1989), 13 Cross Street, Pepperell, Massachusetts, 01463 $12.95
Excellent resource for where routes went and when they were abandoned. Interesting chapters on the histories of some of New England's more famous railroads. Look for an updated edition to be published in 1995.
----------------- *The Rail Lines of Southern New England: A Handbook of Railroad History* (1995), Branchline Press. $22.95.

Krause, John, and Fred Bailey. *Trains of Northern New England,* Quadrant Press Inc. (1977), 19-West 44th Street, New York, NY 10036.

Libby, R. C., and Carol M. Furnee. *Through the Woods to Winnipesaukee: The Story of the Wolfeborough Railroad,* Published by the Boston & Maine Railroad Historical Society, Inc. (1974).

Moody, Linwood W. *The Maine Two Footers: The Story of the Two-Foot Gauge Railroads of Maine,* Howell-North Books (1959), 1150 Parker Street, Berkeley, CA 94710.

Morse, Victor. *36 Miles of Trouble: The Story of the West River Railroad,* Stephen Greene Press (1973), Brattleboro, VT 05301.

Nelligan, Tom. *Bluebirds and Minuteman: Boston & Maine: 1974-1984,* McMillan Publications, Inc. (1986), 2921 Two Paths Drive, Woodridge, IL 60517-4512.

Nelligan, Tom. *The Valley Railroad Story: The Connecticut Valley Line,* Quadrant Press, Inc. (1983), 19 West 44th Street, New York, NY 10036.

Nielsen, Waldo. *Right-of-Way: A Guide to Abandoned Railroads in the United States,* Maverick Publications (1992), P.O. Box 5007, Bend OR 97708. $19.95 Written by the late Mr. Nielsen, this book is credited with sparking interest in the Rails-to-Trails movement. Valuable for its overview of the subject of rail-trails and maps of railroads in each of the United States.

Phelps, George. *New England Rail Album: A Traveling Salesman Remembers the 1930s,* Trans-Anglo (1990), P.O. Box 6444, Glendale, CA 91225.

Nehrich, John. *Milk Train Data Pack,* Published by the Rensselaer Model Railroad (1993), Rensselaer Student Union, Troy, NY 12180-3590.

Nimke, Robert W. *Connecticut River Railroads and Connections,* R.W. Nimke (1995), 36 Old Route 12 North, Westmoreland, NH 03467-4703.
    A ten-volume series on the railroads of Vermont and New Hampshire, with a focus on track layout and industries served.

Shaughnessy, Jim. *Delaware & Hudson,* Howell-North Books (1967), 1150 Parker Street, Berkeley, CA 94710.

Turner, Gregg M., and Melancthon W. Jacobus. *Connecticut Railroads,* The Connecticut Historical Society (1989), One Elizabeth Street, Hartford, CT.

Walker, Mike. *Railroad Atlas of North America,* Steam Powered Publishing (1993), Dawes Road, Dunkirk, Mt.. Faversham, Kent ME 13 9TP. Order for $19.95 through Carstens Publishing Co., P.O.Box 700 Newton, NJ 07860 (201-383-3355). Shows stations, junctions, yards, and tunnels. Original owning company and current owners' names are displayed.

Railroad Historical Societies

Boston & Maine Railroad
Boston & Maine Historical Society
P.O. Box 2936
Middlesex-Essex GMF
Woburn, MA 01888

Central Vermont Railway
Central Vermont Historical Society
John Haropulos
1070 Belmont Street
Manchester, NH 03104

Conrail
Conrail Technical Society
John P. Krattinger
P.O. Box 7140
Garden City, NY 11530

Delaware & Hudson Railway
Bridge Line Historical Society
P.O. Box 7242
Capital Station, Albany, NY 12224

New York Central System
New York Central System Historical Society
P.O. Box 81184
Cleveland, OH 44181-0184

New York, New Haven & Hartford Railroad
New Haven Railroad Historical and Technical Association
Tom Pruchnicki
P.O. Box 122
Wallingford, CT 06492

Rutland Railroad
Rutland Historical Society
P.O. Box 6262
Rutland, VT 05701

Hiking Clubs and Organizations

Appalachian Mountain Club (AMC)
5 Joy Street
Boston, MA 02108
(617)-523-0636

Adirondack Mtn. Club (ADK)
RR3, Box 3055
Lake George, NY 12845
(518)-668-4447

Connecticut Forest & Parks Association
16 Meriden Road
Rockfall, CT 06481
(203)-346-2372

Green Mountain Club (GMC)
RR1, Box 650, Rte 100
Waterbury Center, VT 05677
(802)-244-7037

New York / New Jersey Trail Conference
232 Madison Avenue, #401
New York, NY 10016
(212)-685-9699

North Andover Trail Committee
C/O Conservation Office
120 Main Street
North Andover, MA01845
(508)-682-6483

Pioneer Valley Trail Conference
Bruce Scofield
P.O. Box 561, Amherst, MA 01004
(413)-253-9450

Southern New England Trail Conference
Bill Perry
300 Putnam Hill Road, Sutton, MA 01590
(508)-865-6123

Bicycling Clubs

Bicycle Coalition of Maine
P.O.Box 5275
Augusta, ME 04332-5257
Charles LaFlamme, President
207-646-0635

Bicycle Coalition of Massachusetts
P.O. Box 1015
Cambridge, MA 02142
617-491-RIDE

Charles River Wheelmen
19 Chase Avenue
West Newton, MA 02165

Granite State Wheelmen
83 Londonderry Road
Windham, NH 03087

New England Mountain Bike Association
P.O. Box 380557
Cambridge, MA 02238
508-774-0906

Rails-to-Trails Conservancy
1400 16th St. Suite 300
Washington D.C. 20036
202-797-5400
202-797-5411 (FAX)

Rhode Island Fat Tire Club
245 Old Coach Road
Charlestown, RI 02822
401-364-0786

Seven Hills Wheelmen
P.O. Box 24
Worcester, MA 01606
508-845-5571

NOTES

NOTES

Other Products from New England Cartographics

Maps:

Mt. Tom Reservation Trail Map
Holyoke Range State Park (Eastern Section)
Holyoke Range/Skinner State Park (Western Section)
Mt. Greylock Reservation Trail Map
Mt. Toby Reservation Trail Map
Mt. Wachusett and Leominster State Forest Trail Map
Western Mass. Trail Map Pack (includes six maps listed above)

Quabbin Reservation Guide (available in a water-proof version)
New England Trails (general locator map)
Grand Monadnock Trail Map
Connecticut River Map (in Massachusetts)
Wapack Trail Map
Pocumtuck Ridge Trail Map

Books:

Guide to the Taconic Trail System (in Berkshire County, MA)
Guide to the Metacomet-Monadnock Trail
Hiking the Pioneer Valley (25 circuit hikes)
The Deerfield River Guide
High Peaks of the Northeast

Send for ordering information and current prices to:
New England Cartographics
P.O. Box 9369
North Amherst, MA 01059

Additional copies of **Great Rail-Trails of the Northeast** can be ordered from the publisher for $14.95 (+ $2.00 P & H for the first book and $.75 for each additional book). Telephone orders: **(413) 549-4124.**

ORDER FORM

Additional copies of *Great Rail-Trails of the Northeast* can be purchased directly from the publisher. Send $14.95 (plus $2.00 postage/handling for the first book and $.75 for each additional book) to:

New England Cartographics
PO Box 9369
North Amherst, MA 01059

Please send my order to:

Name_____

Street_____

_____

City_____State_____Zip_____

Master Card --- Visa ---- (circle which card)

Card # _____

Expiration Date _____

Signature _____

Telephone (optional) _____

☐ Please send me ordering information and the price list for products offered by New England Cartographics